Twayne's United States Authors Series

EDITOR OF THIS VOLUME

Warren French

Indiana University

John Ciardi

TUSAS 367

John Ciardi in 1962

JOHN CIARDI

By EDWARD KRICKEL
University of Georgia

TWAYNE PUBLISHERS
A DIVISION OF G. K. HALL & CO., BOSTON

Library of Congress Cataloging in Publication Data

Krickel, Edward Francis.
John Ciardi.

(Twayne's United States authors series ; TUSAS 367)
Bibliography: p. 180–184
Includes index.
1.   Ciardi, John, 1916-   —Criticism and
interpretation.
PS3505.I27Z75   811'.52   80-24902
ISBN 0-8057-7306-1

For
Sallie
and
Edward
and
Elizabeth
and
Mary

Contents

About the Author

Edward Krickel is a member of the Department of English at the University of Georgia. A native of Tennessee, he received his formal education from the University of Tennessee, Peabody College, and Vanderbilt University. He has been a teacher in Arkansas, Tennessee, Kentucky, and South Carolina, in addition to Georgia. In 1972–74, he was acting editor of the *Georgia Review*. His publications include a book of poems, *Segment of a View* (1965).

Preface

John Ciardi has been a prolific man of letters for four decades. His accomplishment is notable as poet—his chief work—critic and essayist, teacher and author of textbooks, translator, and writer of children's books. He has no novels, no plays, no stories (except for two early ones, of which one appeared pseudonymously). But he has thirteen books of poems and thirteen books for children; has translated Dante in three volumes with full scholarly apparatus for teaching and reading; has two books of essays, selected from dozens; has one textbook, revised with a collaborator, and himself collaborated on another; has edited a collection of poems by his contemporaries; has written some twenty to fifty essays a year as a regular columnist for *Saturday Review*. Any professional man of letters might have done as much. Few have, just as few poets have begun their careers as auspiciously as Ciardi. His first book, awarded a Hopwood prize at the University of Michigan, saw publication by a substantial commercial publisher. It and following books were noticed by influential critics and journals and treated with respect by fellow poets and academicians. Most of the instruments agree that Ciardi has occupied a substantial place in the contemporary literary scene. Is he the major poet his publisher claims him to be? There has been no full-scale analysis and appraisal of the work as yet. With a living writer, it may be too soon to determine his place in literature with precision, but for a poet who has aspired to capture in words the real, the authentic, the study of his work has a fascination and worth of its own.

Obviously, if we are to examine the spate of his work, it must be divided in some way, even selected. Two main divisions seem the most reasonable—by type or genre and by chronology. Ciardi is first and foremost a poet; out of this, the rest has grown. Therefore, I have given book-by-book attention to the poems, omitting only the children's verse (which I have read and enjoyed) because of the limitations of space. Those poems examined are of necessity selective, and, in the absence of an official canon, the selection is necessarily my own. Perhaps the choices in this study will aid in the establishment of such a canon. I have by no means commented on all of the good poems or the other ones, either. My method is essentially analytical and descriptive rather than critical, but inevitably criticism has crept in. Because any book by Ciardi includes many of the themes and subjects that all of them have, the thing to emphasize in analyses is both the recurrence and the variations. I think my method is the best way to present Ciardi, but I would not necessarily recommend it for every poet. Also, though I borrow from the prose at will, those volumes do not get individual attention.

The pages on the poetry make an effort to set forth the development of Ciardi's art, theme getting the most attention. The fact that there are recurrences facilitates such points. A poet is not, of course, of interest just for his themes, but for his poems—and any poem is some kind of performance. Ciardi has made this point time and again. Further, a Ciardi book is usually a selection of poems from many available and is thus a kind of performance of its own. At the risk of repetition, I have tried to notice as many poems as possible. How else to give a sense of Ciardi's overall accomplishment? The other chapters are shoots from this main trunk.

One other point. With a living writer, still active, smaller generalizations are preferable to larger ones. Since a living writer is entitled to his privacy except as he reveals it himself, there will be no attempt in this study to go beyond or behind the public record for materials on its subject. This is in accord with Ciardi's recurrent condemnation in his essays of "the simple splendid assumption that the life of the reverie and of the imagination must correspond directly to the factual bones of a man's biography."[1] The former two as made public in the work must be our chief concern. It was Auden who cautioned the poet against writing a formal autobiography on the grounds that his whole poetic stock-in-trade would be expended in the one work —something Ciardi has never done, though he approached it in *Lives of X.* On the other hand, he is preeminently a personal writer. Ciardi's poems, as Miller Williams confirms, are "to a remarkable degree . . . about the experience and knowledge of the man who writes them."[2] The same point had been made by Winfield Townley Scott twenty years earlier: ". . . All of Ciardi's poetry is woven out of the belly of 'personal record.' "[3] In the case of this poet, ever mindful as we must be not to be simple-minded, the poet and the man do seem remarkably close. Williams again confirms: "The poet . . . is the man. . . . Not every poet can appear as himself in his works and interest us in what he is saying about experiences that in a special autobiographical sense are still his."[4] In Ciardi's case, his personal and his poetic worlds lie close together. This is not to regard him as the ultimate authority on himself and his work. He not less than other men and poets is subject to the perils of intention, rationalization, self-justification, or deception. Therefore, readers should not hesitate to disagree with his interpretations of himself, or to see his works for themselves—subject to similar perils. Ciardi, I think, would approve a receptive reader's having his own views.

Any critical approach must seem mechanical, arbitrary, and pallid before a varied and vital body of work such as Ciardi's. The life of art does, no doubt, recede before criticism. However, despite the different faces of his output, one can find patterns in its variety; to grasp them is to increase understanding and to enhance appreciation. The interested reader can be compared to Menelaus grappling with Proteus. If he can hold on tight through the changes of aspect, the true nature of the literary phenomenon John Ciardi is may begin to reveal itself. It is worth the effort.

EDWARD KRICKEL

University of Georgia

Acknowledgments

In writing this study, I am especially grateful to my wife Sallie for her faith, her encouragement, and her practical solutions to problems I could not solve for myself.

Mr. Warren French, Twayne field editor, gave indispensable help in putting a much longer manuscript into a publishable form.

Without the time off from teaching that the University of Georgia and its Department of English made possible, I would have been unable to do the study at all.

Mr. John Ciardi holds the reprint rights to all of his works. All quotations are by his kind permission.

Chronology

1916   Born June 24, John Anthony Ciardi, in Boston, Massachusetts, the fourth child and only son of Concetta DeBenedictis and Carminantonio Ciardi.

1919   Father killed in automobile accident, on the way to a company picnic.

1921   Family moved to Medford, seven miles out of Boston. John attended the public schools.

1933   Worked for a year after high school, then entered Bates College, Lewiston, Maine, to take prelaw.

1935   Transferred to Tufts College in February.

1938   A.B., *magna cum laude*, 1938.

1938–   Entered the University of Michigan on a tuition scholar-
1939   ship. First important recognition as poet, by winning the first prize in poetry of the Avery Hopwood Awards, and stipend of $1,200.

1940   First book published, *Homeward to America*.

1940–   Instructor in English at University of Kansas City, in
1942   Missouri.

1942   Enlisted United States Army Air Force.

1943   Oscar Blumenthal Prize, *Poetry Magazine*.

1944   Eunice Tietjens Memorial Prize, *Poetry Magazine*.

1945   Combat duty as gunner on B-29 in air offensive against Japan. Discharged October 1945, with rank of Technical Sergeant, also Air Medal and Oak Leaf Cluster.

1946   Returned to Kansas City teaching position for one semester. Married on July 28 to Myra Judith Hostetter. Levinson Prize, *Poetry Magazine*. Briggs-Copeland Instructor in English, Harvard University.

1947   *Other Skies*. Joined staff of Bread Loaf Writers Conference as lecturer on poetry.

1948   Assistant Professor, Harvard, 1948–53.

1949   Entered into association with Jacob Steinberg of Twayne Publishers and became Poetry Editor, later Executive Editor. *Live Another Day*.

1950   Edited *Mid-Century American Poets*.

1950– On leave from Harvard. Lectured on poetry at Salzburg
1951   Seminar in American Studies. *From Time to Time.*

1952   Phi Beta Kappa poem, Harvard. Elected Fellow, American Academy of Arts and Sciences. Daughter Myra Judith Ciardi born March 19.

1953   Son John Lyle Pritchett Ciardi born May 2. Lecturer in Creative Writing, Rutgers University. Associate professor of English, 1954–56; professor, 1956–61.

1954   Translation of Dante's *Inferno.* Son Benn Anthony Ciardi born December 25.

1955   *As If: Poems New and Selected.* Harriet Monroe Memorial Award. Director of Bread Loaf Writers' Conference; resigned 1972.

1956   In January began his long-continued journalistic association with Norman Cousins and the *Saturday Review,* which lasted until 1977. *Prix de Rome* of American Academy of Arts and Letters in Rome.

1957   Elected Fellow, National Institute of Arts and Letters.

1958   *I Marry You.* President, College English Association.

1959   *39 Poems.* First juvenile, *The Reason for the Pelican. How Does a Poem Mean?*

1960   D. Litt., Tufts. *Scrappy the Pup.*

1961   *I Met a Man. The Man Who Sang the Sillies. In the Stoneworks.* Dante's *Purgatorio.* Resigned professorship at Rutgers.

1961– Served as host of *Accent,* an educational program for CBS
1962   television.

1962   *The Wish-Tree. You Read to Me, I'll Read to You. In Fact.*

1963   D. Hum., Wayne State University. *John J. Plenty and Fiddler Dan. Dialogue with an Audience.*

1964   LL.D., Ursinus College. L.H.D., Kalamazoo College. *You Know Who. Person to Person. Poetry: A Closer Look* (with James M. Reid and Laurence Perrine).

1965   *The King Who Saved Himself from Being Saved.*

1966   *This Strangest Everything. The Monster Den.*

1967   *An Alphabestiary.*

1970   L.H.D., Bates College. *Someone Could Win a Polar Bear.* Dante's *Paradiso.*

1971   L.H.D., Washington University. L.H.D., Ohio Wesleyan College. *Lives of X.* D.Litt., University of Delaware.

Chronology

1972   *Manner of Speaking.*
1974   *The Little That Is All.*
1975   *Fast and Slow. How Does a Poem Mean?* (rev. ed. with Miller Williams).
1977   *The Divine Comedy.*
1978   *Limericks: Too Gross* (with Isaac Asimov).

CHAPTER 1

The World of a Poet

THE factual and public part of John Ciardi's life and career is the easily recognized source both for much of the poetry and most of the journalism. Certain recurring attitudes may be read from the experiences.

Ciardi was born on June 24, 1916, in Boston, Massachusetts. His parents were Carminantonio and Concetta DeBenedictus Ciardi from the vicinity of Avellino in Italy, near Naples, born, respectively, in Campobasso and Naples; the father had immigrated in 1890.[1] John was the only son among the four children. The Italian background, with its Catholicism, the double culture of Old World and New, the name inevitably mispronounced by those of Anglo-Saxon stock and bias, the relatives who never became entirely naturalized—these and related themes are repeated to the point of near obsession in the mature writer's work. Painful many of them were, by his own account, but they supplied him with a rich subject matter and a perspective. However much the mature writer might participate in the dominant culture of his own time and country, there is always —intellectually, at least—some detachment, a sense of the imperfectly naturalized, something like an intellectual equivalent constructed in pride by the mature man to justify the unreconciled circumstances of childhood and youth. When in 1919 the father was killed in a freak automobile accident, the tragedy supplied another subject for later poetic exploration of its manifold aspects and significances—the search for the father Ciardi was too young to remember but whose name was kept alive by an unforgetting wife. The family moved to Medford, Massachusetts, in 1921, where the boy attended the public schools.

Ciardi's life and work cannot be separated from his experience with American higher education. He prepared himself for a career as teacher and devoted nearly twenty years to the profes-

sion. Though he put full-time teaching behind him when he
resigned a Rutgers University professorship in 1961, he kept the
directorship of the Bread Loaf summer writing conference until
1972, and he has returned more than once for short-time stints in
universities, for example Wisconsin at Milwaukee in 1963 and the
University of Florida in 1973. Though Ciardi is severely critical of
American education, more of teachers and students than of the
institution itself, he has been very much shaped by it and, on
balance, much the beneficiary, though any poet is largely self-
taught, or likely feels he is. Ciardi is as natural a teacher as Ezra
Pound, who lasted only one term in college teaching, with an
equally large sense of obligation to teach his generation, to teach
the young, to teach the so-called literate public their limitations
and how they may be improved. Any teacher ought to recognize,
especially in Ciardi's essays, the basic positions and even many of
the devices as coming from the classroom, for example the clown-
ing, buffoonery, wheedling, irony, the reducing of positions to
humorous absurdity, though few may claim to equal Ciardi's wit
or verve or, through it all, passionate love of language and its
possibilities. In a serious statement—and these predominate despite the wit—Ciardi tells a teacher that his "duty is to teach
method of inquiry, ideas, and criteria."[2] His journalistic career
has several times become controversial because of the vehemence
with which he has applied these precepts. For like Pound he has
often sought to redeem the times through art, and, also like
Pound, he has not hesitated to instruct the nation. It was these
controversies that brought him truly to national attention
—critical essays rather than poems.

I   *Higher Education: Tufts and Holmes, Michigan and Cowden*

The poet's formal beginnings with higher education are in-
auspicious, even in part obscure. Olga Peragallo states that, after
his graduation from Medford High School in 1933, he "had to
wait another year before he could accumulate enough money to
go to College . . . then entered Bates College, and a year and a
half later he transferred to Tufts College."[3] Ciardi's own note of
1955 states: "In 1933 I entered Bates College, Lewiston, Maine,
transferred to Tufts College in the middle of my sophomore
year."[4] Any teacher looking at these statements might sense

vagaries, given further credence by the anecdote John Holmes told in both of his notes on the poet, about a kindly Bates professor of Latin who informed Ciardi "with old-world courtesy that he was highest among those who failed to pass the course." Holmes, who should have known, said that Ciardi "cheerfully threw away a freshman year at Bates College" and was given another chance, at Tufts, because it was near his home.[5] Ciardi himself recalled of the Bates experience that he had gone there "looking for something and got myself moralized at / and knew that wasn't what I'd been looking for" (*Lives of X*, 86). And he also said he went to college to study law and took so many literature courses he was not employable.[6]

What that something more nearly was he found in John Holmes, "just the teacher one insane adolescent had been starved for."[7] The influence of Holmes was fortunate and profound —"my teacher / father, friend, and host to my blowfly eggs . . . " (*Lives of X*, 85). Perhaps partly as a result of this influence, Ciardi graduated *magna cum laude* five years after entering college. He wrote for the campus magazine and acted in student dramatic productions, and participated in no other campus activities.[8]

It is a turning point in the development of every budding young intellectual or artist when he finds his first real master. And he is lucky if in his full maturity he can recall the experience with gratitude. Holmes was the first such experience for Ciardi, as Roy W. Cowden of Michigan was to be the second. Both have remained emblems of the good teacher for someone who can have claims entered on his own behalf. Ciardi remembered in 1961 how Holmes had not only cared, which "caring only begins a teacher's work," but as a practicing poet he knew about poems from the inside, unlike the usual historical scholar of the time. In addition to this kind of knowledge, exactly the kind young Ciardi felt he needed, Holmes had in abundance the qualities every great teacher must have—"generosity, the gift of articulation, and the power to elicit enthusiasm."[9]

Ciardi describes the sort of thing Holmes did for him. He had turned in a poem for his teacher to praise—"What else do we mean when we ask for criticism?"—only to get it back with a sharp marginal criticism: " 'All right; you're haunted. When does it haunt me?' " The lesson was profound:

I was never pretty again in any mirror.
I began to learn music comes off the piano
ten-fingered from eighty-eight keys, and that all the god
that yearns in pain speaks that arithmetic
or only burbles. If that seems little to learn,
I haven't finished learning it. . . . (*Lives of X*, 87)

The teacher responded equally to his talented pupil: "Teachers of creative writing get such students as John Ciardi once in a decade, even if they are lucky, and it was obvious that while he scarcely needed ordinary academic instruction or encouragement, he valued it, and it was equally obvious that nothing at all could or would stop him from writing."[10]

Their relationship, as Holmes described it not long after the time, was "closer than that of instructor and student: it was that of poet and poet, finally that of competitor and competitor, almost. That is as it should be. We were at one another's homes constantly, and deeply involved in our own lives and those of the people closest to us. That means that Ciardi was maturing rapidly, closing the gap in years, if there was ever a gap, between us."[11] Ciardi's first book bore the dedication: "To John Holmes." There can be no doubt that young Ciardi found his direction at Tufts and that Holmes figured prominently in the experience.

Every human experience is flawed. For all Ciardi's later success, the Bates experience was a failure, and at Tufts "he missed election to Phi Beta Kappa by a few tenths of a point, and was not made happy that his friends made it."[12] Though he did graduate *magna cum laude*, he still in *Lives of X* resents a boy who was *summa*. And the experience with Holmes was complicated at the personal level. Was it not alluded to in Holmes's phrase "deeply involved in our own lives and those of the people closest to us"? What more is needed to complicate a friendship than a woman? In "The Highest Place in Town" from *Lives of X*, Ciardi recounts such a difficulty between himself and his mentor. After a painful admission involving a woman Ciardi had had sexual relations with ("that bed was mine") but whom Holmes intended to marry, "we never again were friends."(She is presumably the suicide described in the same poem.) Nevertheless, the two paid each other graceful and no doubt sincere compliments over the years, and after Holmes's death Ciardi returned to Tufts to fill a chair named in his honor. Every young poet has such a mentor whom he betrays and grows beyond by conforming to his own nature and then cherishes forever, along with his ambiguous youth; so life proceeds.

Very likely at Holmes's suggestion, the budding young poet looked for a graduate program in which he could further his study of poetry and chose Michigan because of the Hopwood Awards given there. He set out over a year in advance to win the prize for poetry. There was surely more pride in his ability than youthful bravado, and also—a recurrent double motive, by his own account—he needed the money. In a note for the *Tuftonian: The Magazine of Tufts College* in 1944, Professor Roy W. Cowden, then director of the Hopwood Awards, quotes Ciardi's letter of inquiry, dated early in October 1937. The note was respectful, formal, and self-conscious; on one point it was firm and unequivocally clear: ". . . My interest in writing is entirely given to poetry." Strangely, in a graduate academic context, the professor "pondered over the word Ciardi trying it this way and that and wondering how to pronounce it."[13] This small drama repeated in private the experience of a lifetime. The mature poet dealt with it explicitly in "A Knothole in Spent Time," in *Lives of X*. The problem of a name and an identity, an almost ubiquitous theme in Ciardi's poetry, no doubt had its start in Medford's Craddock School on Summer Street. The mispronunciation of his name and what that connoted for him lasted through Tufts. It was not until his arrival at Michigan by bus seventeen years later that he felt he had escaped the false appellation. The escape was by the skin of his teeth, as Cowden's admission shows.

When, in October 1938, Cowden read the first of Ciardi's poems with all of a teacher's mixed hope that they will be good and fear that they will not, he was impressed: "Have you ever heard lines like these before?" He was moved by "the vitality and freshness of the language" to conclude, "I think this year we have a poet coming here to Michigan."[14]

Ciardi became one of six students in Cowden's seminar who were working on book-length manuscripts. In that class, according to Cowden, the young man began to write the poems that eventually made up his first book, *Homeward to America*, though Holmes said Ciardi "took with him from Tufts the essential poetry of that first volume" and "re-wrote a great deal of it between award and publication."[15] Good teachers like their students to grow and develop. Cowden recalled, as one of his own

notable experiences of that year, "John Ciardi's growing awareness of the quality of a line that belonged to him and growing
recognition of the lines in which he fell from his own way into the
paths of others. . . ."[16]

Some thirty years later, Ciardi remembered, somewhat lightly,
Professor Cowden as a great teacher, even though the weekly
seminar was a "torture" to the young poet: "In love I could not
bring myself to cut it; in nature, I could not keep myself awake in
it as he droned over manuscript revisions in Hardy." But in the
once-a-week individual conferences, where master and neophyte
went over the neophyte's latest work, Cowden would point uner-
ringly to the trouble spots in the manuscript. Unable to remember
a word his professor said, Ciardi can still see "that dowsing
finger . . . come down on the page at times." Together with
Holmes, then, Cowden became one of Ciardi's "masters of the
million particulars."[17] *Other Skies*, Ciardi's second book, is
dedicated to "Roy W. Cowden, gratefully."

In 1944, Holmes recalled that he "never had the slightest doubt
that John would attain distinction in Ann Arbor." Because the
young man had little money at Michigan, he arranged to send the
cheapest kind of form telegram to his former teacher by which the
latter would know a Hopwood prize had been won of a hundred
dollars or possibly more. Instead, Holmes remembered, there
came "a full paid wire, saying, 'Ring out wild bells twelve hundred bucks.' "[18] The calculation that sent young Ciardi to
Michigan had paid off. A career was underway.

II   *Kansas City to Harvard to Rutgers and Out*

The year at Michigan completed, Ciardi set out for the West
Coast by car to discover America, characteristically for himself.
This his parents had been obliged to do earlier—"But there will
be no Americas discovered by analogy," as the opening poem in
Homeward to America asserts. While visiting the University of
Kansas City he got an appointment as instructor of English, and
in January of 1940 the "new-minted instructor" began his first
teaching.[19] Still another career was begun. If Holmes had it right,
that first job was "on his own terms . . . meaning that he worked
one term and came home and wrote poetry the rest of the
year. . . ."[20] The luck of "Lucky John" was running good.

A certain disillusionment set in no later than the summer session of 1940, when he taught modern poetry to a class of schoolteachers.[21] However, he continued in Missouri until he enlisted in the Air Corps in 1942. After military discharge in October 1945, Ciardi returned to Kansas City for one semester. Before leaving, he took another fateful step in his life which has affected his work: he married Judith Hostetter, a farm girl from Frankford, Missouri. His next appointment was at Harvard as a Briggs-Copeland Instructor in English, and promotion to Briggs-Copeland Assistant Professor in 1948.[22] Holmes explains the significance of the title: "The Briggs Copeland appointments are for young men of already distinguished literary achievement, and have a limit of five years, without re-appointment to the Harvard faculty thereafter."[23] Ciardi put in the years from 1953 to 1961 teaching at Rutgers. He was a "full-chicken professor of English" with tenure when he resigned in June 1961.[24] Interleaved in these experiences is the association with the Bread Loaf Writers' Conference, a summer session of two weeks' duration. Ciardi joined the staff in 1947 and succeeded Theodore Morrison as its director in 1955; he held that post until his resignation in 1972. Ciardi was voted by students "the most popular professor at Harvard." And Holmes characterized his teaching as "forceful, brilliant, and a rare combination of scholarliness and earthy humanity."[25] This judgment could easily be confirmed by the many auditors who have attended Ciardi's innumerable public lectures.

III *World War II*

The course of any young person's life will be affected if not altered by the war of his time, no matter what his relation to it. Ciardi was no exception. He served three years in the Air Corps and saw "combat service 1944–45 as aerial gunner on B-29. Based on Saipan." He was at the time of his discharge a technical sergeant.[26] One notices an oddity immediately. From the date of enlistment in 1942 to combat duty in 1944 is a long time. Holmes gave an explanation: "He trained first as a navigator, but for reasons that had nothing to do with his ability, did not receive his lieutenant's bars. He was re-trained as a bombadier and flew some fifteen missions. . . ."[27] It seems unlikely that Ciardi failed to make the grade as a bombardier or else, making it, trained additionally as the gunner he says he was. Cowden is probably more accurate when he wrote in 1944 that Ciardi was a "central control gunner of a B-29."[28] Holmes is clearly wrong, perhaps because of a cavalier attitude toward the military in which gunner, navigator, and bombardier were equally abstract, unreal, and very likely absurd. He seems to have cared more that his protégé had achieved only the rank of technical sergeant instead of lieutenant.

Regardless, war is the central experience of *Other Skies* "by an accident of chaos," the author said. Holmes found the war poems "remarkable, among other excellences, for using so much of his air-base experience," as well as experiences from his return to civilian life.[29] Though war and the military dominate *Other Skies* and war or military poems appear in nearly every other Ciardi book, one feels the permanent part of the young poet's experience was not war itself, but rather something else. He found institutionalized a massive and all-powerful machine, combining genius and stupidity, rationally devised yet devoted to the devilish ends of murder and destruction. In a sense, this was a grown-up repetition of that first day in Craddock School when the teacher couldn't even pronounce his name. He saw institutionalized authority less competent than the individual, who counted for nothing at all. And a poet, unlike a soldier, is an individual before he is anything else. That "Lucky John" did *not* achieve commissioned rank may have been the good fortune which only time could demonstrate. The detachment Sgt. Ciardi had from the seats of power was greater than what Lt. Ciardi would have had.

IV   *Bread Loaf: Life and Contacts*

When Ciardi returned to civilian life, the Bread Loaf Writers' Conference no doubt gave him the opportunity to pay back in the best way a small part of the debt he owed to Holmes for the individual attention to his fledgling work. And what teacher could ask for a better situation than to teach interested students who had actually qualified for admission to the class?

The director invites each year's staff, and among those during Ciardi's time were William Sloane, longtime participant, and since 1955 the director of Rutgers University Press, which has been the publisher of Ciardi's poems for adults since that year (though the translation of the *Inferno* came out through Rutgers the year before), as well as *Manner of Speaking*, the collection of his *Saturday Review* columns, in 1972. Ciardi had met Sloane when the latter worked for the publisher of *Homeward to America*. Still another is Miller Williams, dedicatee of *Lives of X*, whose help is there gratefully acknowledged and who had earlier edited the selection of his poems intended as a college text, called *The Achievement of John Ciardi*. Still another is Maxine Kumin, whom Ciardi has praised and reviewed in the pages of *Saturday Review*.

V *Twayne and* Saturday Review

Two other associations have provided milestones in the Ciardi career. They are Jacob Steinberg of Twayne Publishers and Norman Cousins of the *Saturday Review*. Ciardi became a Twayne editor in 1949, the year Twayne published his third volume of poems, *Live Another Day*. He later became executive editor. Money, outlets for his works and influence, and even a kind of tough-minded idealism were likely involved. Among the issues of this union were an introduction to *Witches Three*, edited by his Bread Loaf friend Fletcher Pratt in 1951, an introduction to an Italian cookbook in 1953, and ghostwriting the autobiography of jazzman Sidney Bechet. Such diversities boded well for the future columnist in the *Saturday Review*.

In 1949, so ran an advertising squib, "Twayne announces a full scale program devoted to contemporary poetry," with the motto "to serve the poet, to serve the audience." In those days before the reign of King Paperback, Twayne pointed out that so-called major publishers issued few "volumes of verse" (Cowden had noted that Ciardi referred to his interest in poetry rather than in verse) and entered a claim for itself as "a significant force in modern letters, and a distinct contribution to American culture." Part of the program was an "Annual Twayne First Book Contest." These intentions are as admirable as they are redolent of youthful high hopes—and almost as certainly doomed to disappointment. The only American publishers up to that time who had shown a similar interest in contemporary poetry and were willing (or able) to take the risk were New Directions with its Poet of the Month series, the much smaller Alan Swallow press, and the still smaller and much less discriminating Press of James C. Decker of Prairie City, Iowa, self-styled as "the largest publishing

house in America devoted exclusively to poetry," under whose
auspices Ciardi had published thirteen poems in the 1941 collection *New Poets*.

The 1949 Twayne winner was Marshall Schacht with *Finger-
board*, bearing a preface by the recently deceased F. O. Mat-
thiessen; and the 1950 winner, "selected by Archibald
MacLeish," was *Immediate Sun* by Rosemary Thomas. Whether
the scheme originated with Ciardi, Steinberg, the two together,
or otherwise hardly matters. The signs of Ciardi's taste are
everywhere in the series. By 1950, the year the excellent Ciardi-
edited *Mid-Century American Poets* came out, the Twayne
Library of Modern Poetry included two books by John Holmes;
two by Merrill Moore (whom Ciardi later acknowledged as his
good friend); T. Weiss and Radcliffe Squires, both to review
Ciardi's work in the future; Selwyn S. Schwartz, earlier published by Decker; E. L. Mayo, included in *Mid-Century
American Poets*; and Dilys Bennett Laing, later promoted by
Ciardi in an essay, and who gave him a tough-minded review.

Lingering in the poetic air of 1950 were the issues of the controversy stirred up by Robert Hillyer and Norman Cousins in the
pages of the *Saturday Review of Literature* over the award of the
first Bollingen prize to Ezra Pound's *Pisan Cantos* while the poet
was under indictment for treason and officially declared insane.
The supervising agency for the award was the Library of Congress. (The highly approving reader response to Hillyer's two ar-
ticles might have shown the futility of the Twayne Library of
Modern Poetry, had anyone thought to bring the two together.)
With the retrospect of twenty-five years and with poetry placed
well up in the hierarchy of cultural values, the choice of the *Pisan
Cantos* seems vindicated; Hillyer and Cousins appear to have
been essentially wrong, and certainly spiteful if by no means
despicable. Ciardi—one hopes ever respectful of poetic achievement rather than equivocating—in 1950 characterized the award
as "dubious but still partly defensible." The big issue, insofar as it
concerned poetry, seemed to be whether modern poetry was in-
telligible. Poetry had been put on trial.

Ciardi's *Mid-Century American Poets* testified for the defense,
it looks now, yet without giving offense to Cousins; at least he
became Cousins's poetry editor and contributing columnist beginning in 1956. The anthology gave him the opportunity to assess

the contemporary scene and his own place in it. The long shadows of Eliot and Pound touched the collection in many places, as the ghost of Hamlet's father touched the prince.

Fifteen poets were contributors—including the editor in his role as poet—all of them "the poets who have generally been recognized as having done their best work in the last 10 to 15 years, and who were not widely recognized before that time." The others were Richard Wilbur, Peter Viereck, Muriel Rukeyser, Theodore Roethke (whom Ciardi had met through Holmes while still at Tufts), Karl Shapiro, Winfield Townley Scott, John Frederick Nims (later a Bread Loaf colleague), E. L. Mayo, Robert Lowell, Randall Jarrell, John Holmes, Richard Eberhart, Elizabeth Bishop, and Delmore Schwartz.

The "simple principle" of the volume was "to gather together poems reasonably representative of the best work of a generation of poets, and to have each poet preface his poems with a guide to the reader's better understanding of his work and its intent."[30] The poets chose their own poems, from six to thirteen (Ciardi had eleven). As a center, the editor supplied a list of twelve questions for each poet to answer in relation to his own work. The rationale for the questionnaire was that after time's selectivity, say in twenty years, we would not need the poets' answers, but "until time has made clear to us (and to them) their whole intent . . . the poets themselves are likely to be their own best guides to themselves." The answers varied in length from one to fifteen pages; Ciardi's own was eight. The world was younger then and the idea of poets' commenting on their own work was relatively novel and had not yet become a tedious substitute for the work.

Ciardi's association with the *Saturday Review* and its editor Norman Cousins eventually enabled him to leave the "planned poverty" of academic life.[31] The journal published its first piece by him in December 1949 under the title "What Does It Take to Enjoy a Poem?" The title was changed editorially, as he noted when he reprinted it in *Dialogue with an Audience* (1963), from "What Does It Take to Read a Poem?"[32] His first poem for *Saturday Review* appeared in April 1956, shortly before he became poetry editor. It was "For Bernard DeVoto," in commemoration of the former editor of the journal, who also had been Ciardi's colleague at Bread Loaf. His second essay for the journal came in

1950 on the occasion of the death of Edna St. Vincent Millay and precipitated the first of the controversies which soon brought him to national attention.

Ciardi, in Europe for a year, received a cable from the editors asking him for a summary of Millay's poetic career. He received the cable late on Friday afternoon; his copy had to be dispatched by airmail on Monday morning. Despite an eight-hour search in London, he was unable to find any of her work that he might reread or use to check his quotations. Thus he was obliged to write the piece from memory of the youthful time when he "had read Millay with real passion." At the last minute, in an embassy library, he was able to check only a few of the quotations before dispatching his hasty piece with the caution that quotations must be checked in New York. The essay appeared in print with several inaccurate quotations intact, however, and readers were quick to respond with corrections and angry disagreement with his forthright judgments. Curiously, the author himself did not know of this small controversy until, in searching through the files of the *Saturday Review* preparatory to putting together *Dialogue with an Audience*, he found the correspondence.[33] Immediately he was struck "by the fact that the early letters were identical in their terms, tone, and preconceptions with the letters of protest I later received."[34] (One might suspect many were written by the same people.) There in miniature was a preview of things to come, with the added irony of the author's ignorance of the sparks he had struck.

Ciardi had joined the staff of the *Saturday Review* as poetry editor in May 1956, ending a six-year search for a successor to William Rose Benét, who had died in 1950 and whose job had been filled in an acting capacity by Amy Loveman, who had herself died in 1955. Editor Cousins had admired several essays by Ciardi in the *Nation* during the early 1950s, finding them "crisp, articulate, provocative."[35] Trouble began immediately.

Asked to set a poetry policy for the *Saturday Review*, Ciardi walked into a new editor's nightmare in the form of 213 poems accepted for publication, not one of which he would have taken. Since the journal used poems as fillers, these amounted to a two-year supply. With Cousins's reluctant permission, Ciardi, after first offering to resign, sent back over two hundred of these poems with a letter explaining his position. Thus, as he told it, "Before I had published a word as SR's Poetry Editor, within two weeks of the return of the poems, I had a cardboard carton full of letters written between rage and anguish."[36] The essential difference between himself and most of the protesters Ciardi put down to the difference between "a disciplined and an undisciplined aesthetic."[37]

Soon Ciardi became a staff columnist for the *Saturday Review*. His regular column, usually a page in length, at first appeared approximately fifty times a year in the weekly magazine, under the title "Manner of Speaking." The issue of April 15, 1961, bore the first. Cousins in 1967 said that Ciardi wrote "mostly . . . about poetry and his experiences as editor, critic, and lecturer. But he also writes about other things that excite or infuriate him—all the way from the mysteries of fine bourbon to pilots who ditch their planes over population centers."[38]

When in July 1971 the *Saturday Review* was sold by Norton Simon, Inc., to John Veronis and Nicholas Charney, it had a circulation of 662,000.[39] In the midst of many changes, Cousins resigned, despite his thirty-one years as editor and onetime owner. Shortly, he founded *World*. Evidently there were disputes between the old crowd and the new gang. Ciardi soon followed Cousins to *World*, contributing the same kind of column under the new title "As I Was Saying"—with presumably the rest of the saying implied, "before I was so rudely interrupted." Ciardi's last column for *Saturday Review* was not printed, "for reasonable cause," as he explained the matter when it appeared for its first time in print under the title "Goodbye" as the last essay in the book *Manner of Speaking*.

When the *Saturday Review* under Veronis filed for bankruptcy on April 25, 1973, and Cousins to his delight was asked to take over the reorganization of the journal, he combined it with *World* under the title of *Saturday Review/World*. Ciardi resumed his column and title "Manner of Speaking," very likely to *his* delight. The last of these columns appeared in the issue of Sept. 3, 1977.

Ciardi stirred up his biggest controversy with his deliberately harsh, negative review of Anne Morrow Lindbergh's traditional and sentimental *The Unicorn* in January 1957. The readers' attack upon Ciardi was so overwhelming that Cousins himself felt obliged to enter the debate: "Truth to tell, I had been drawn into the affair emotionally, as had everyone else, and didn't need much urging to do a piece. It was, I suppose, something of a straddle. . . ."[40] Cousins's essay "John Ciardi and the Readers"[41] showed him to be closer to his subscribers in poetic values than to his poetry editor. Straddle or not, it caused a "furious" Ciardi to "quit cold, though my letter (from Rome, as it happened) was hot enough." One presumes there was an eventual compromise; at least Ciardi said, "We patched that one up with a careful treaty," which did not preclude later squabbles "over *Saturday Review* policy." Evidently, the treaty confined Ciardi to his column, in which criticism is incidental and definitely personal.

Ciardi precipitated other controversies with his pieces in the *Saturday Review*. In the fall of the momentous year of 1957, the journal published an article by Lord Dunsany, "The Poets Fail in Their Duty." It had been submitted to Cousins by the author's agent. From the editor's desk it went to that of the poetry editor with a recommendation to accept it. "Not while I am Poetry Editor," came back the reply. Ciardi's logic was that if the piece appeared without a rebuttal, that would imply editorial approval. With the consent of Cousins and of Dunsany's literary agent, the piece led off the issue of October 19, 1957, and was followed by Ciardi's "The Poet's Duty to Poetry." Dunsany died on October 25 at the age of seventy-nine, without ever seeing Ciardi's reply. Some readers accused the ever-vigorous poetry editor of "having killed an old man."[42] It was not possible to continue the debate.

In the name of clarity and the poet's duty to make himself understood by the audience, Dunsany had launched a vigorous attack on certain of the principles of modern verse that had been first set forth by the Imagists forty-five years before. Essentially he seemed to want message and melody and high seriousness. He particularly seemed to dislike Cummings and Eliot and saw little difference between them. One thinks that in particular he did not like American idiom. In speaking for tradition and implying it was the immemorial tradition of poetry, he spoke for not much more than a certain mode of Victorian verse. Poetry, submitted to his strictures, would be a much-diminished thing.

In reprinting both expostulation and reply in *Dialogue with an Audience*, Ciardi added that he had found the old man's "views as repugnant as they were firm" and regarded Dunsany as "a pernicious influence."[43] Replying, Ciardi, himself in no way an enemy to clarity, attacked the illogic of Dunsany's approach and the lack of accuracy in his quotations. He was no doubt right that

his antagonist's "imagination was formed in another time and attuned to respond to other attitudes and devices."[44] The exchange,
however, did not bring Ciardi to any new formulation of his own
principles. He came out for logic, honesty, expert technical
knowledge, and unfortunately in passing attributed Verdi's
"Caro Nome" to *La Traviata* rather than *Rigoletto*, a slip which
watchdog readers were quick to spot. Ciardi's reply to Dunsany,
though sound, did not show him to best advantage. Reader
response ranged from strong approval to strong disapproval,
through the hurt and puzzled to wit so rare and personal that it
communicated nothing. Presumably, Cousins wrote the Editor's
Note that said of the late Dunsany, "He was a good friend of, and
to, *The Saturday Review* for three decades. The editors have the
highest respect for him and his work."[45]

Less than a year later came still another controversy, this time
because Ciardi gave a close reading, within his own critical
framework, of Robert Frost's "Stopping by Woods on a Snowy
Evening." He was concerned explicitly with *how* the poem
achieved its meaning. Any teacher of literature may undertake
such a task on any class day and think nothing of it, though
Ciardi's essay is a superior example, beyond what students may
hope to get most of the time. The replies from readers, some of
them by well-known authors, are also within the daily experience
of teachers of literature, though without the mitigation that the
attackers are famous. Basically, they are the people who oppose
analysis of poems on the grounds that it impairs the reader's appreciation of the beauty of the work. As Ciardi put it, "what
emerges as the enemy is the very act of attempted analysis."[46]
This is the dragon that Cleanth Brooks and Robert Penn Warren,
as much as anybody, slew years before in their epoch-making
textbook *Understanding Poetry*; yet evidently the teeth of this
particular monster grow in every soil and clime and produce an
annual crop, again as any teacher can attest. And yet, once more,
Ciardi is quintessentially in the right. Perhaps it is the vigor and
confidence of Ciardi's manner that has offended readers and
moved them to—usually—less than satisfactory, largely emotional replies. As a peroration he gave what amounts to a kind of
explanation of how a poem becomes a classic, a kind of modern
equivalent of Arnold's touchstone theory: "And thus, finally, in
every truly good poem, 'How does it mean?' must always be
answered 'Triumphantly.' Whatever the poem 'is about,' *how* it

means is always how Genesis means: the word become a form, and the form become a thing, and—when the becoming is true—the thing become a part of the knowledge and experience of the race forever."[47]

It is obvious that Ciardi and Cousins have not been of one mind on every issue. Nowhere was this more apparent than in the latter's editorial at the time of the *Unicorn* controversy, "John Ciardi and the Readers." Acknowledging that the Lindbergh review had provoked "the biggest storm of reader protest in the thirty-three-year history of *The Saturday Review*," Cousins tried to answer the questions that had been raised about his editorial policy and procedure. Ciardi had told his editor of his intention to "write a highly critical review" of the book, and was told in reply that, together with other department heads, "he would have direct access to the columns of the magazine" and could count on editorial support for "his right to unobstructed critical opinions. . . ." Interpreted, however, "this did not mean he could count on our automatic support for his views." Cousins admitted that he occasionally published reviews of "books or the other arts" which gave him "the greatest personal pain" because of his "total disagreement." Nevertheless, he felt it necessary as the editor of "an independent journal of criticism" to build a collection of critics "with integrity, authority, vigor, and a point of view." Rarely, he did dissent by means of an editorial. In the *Unicorn* case, Cousins revealed his inadequate understanding of poetry. He thought Ciardi's method of appraising Mrs. Lindbergh's book would be "better adapted to the measurement of prose than poetry." In particular, he found fault with "applying a rigorous test of meaning to each phrase, by insisting on precision in punctuation, by X-raying the intent of the author throughout. . . ." Further, "the important questions about a poem are not limited to its word-by-word or line-by-line content or structure." Cousins evidently espoused a sentimentalized kind of Deweyan aesthetic of art as experience, syruped up with the genteel sentimentality his poetry editor had taken for public problem number one.

Cousins followed fawning praise of the lady whose work was in question, with an *ad hominem* justification of his vigorous poetry editor, in which he denied that he "intended to chastise Mr. Ciardi." One assumes Cousins to be sincere and not just politic with paying subscribers. One further perceives that, far from educating the *Saturday Review* readers, Ciardi had failed to educate his editor-in-chief. Here, if anything, was one more lesson in disillusionment for Ciardi, if he needed it. Looking back, Cousins in 1967 could say of the Ciardi-Lindbergh controversy that "what is important is that poetry and values in literary criticism had come into national focus."[48] Curiously, this is what his poetry editor, with an even longer perspective of history, had hoped to achieve.

Cousins showed himself more nearly in the "purple trunks" of the champion in another editorial on his poetry editor that was, however, provoked from the outside. No doubt more because Ciardi was a national columnist for a magazine with a large circulation and thus a kind of celebrity than because he was a poet, he was a regular lecturer on the college circuit, making fall and spring tours. He gave details of one such tour in 1968 that extended two weeks at a stretch from March through May, with some breaks; it is probably typical. It was booked by an agent. In 1964 he admitted he was "paid well over $1,000 . . . to give a spiel not much different from the spiel I gave in another town last night and from the one I shall give in still another town tomorrow night and so on. . . ." (In one of his columns Ciardi said he grossed $180,000 in a two-year period.) He was quite popular on the circuit until his "virtual retirement from lecturing" in the fall of 1969. According to a headnote to an extended "Manner of Speaking" column in 1970, "Recently the House Internal Security Committee (HISC) polled American colleges and compiled a report on who was traveling the college circuit and how much each man was paid. On October 14, ignoring a court order against releasing its report to the press, HISC published a list of alleged 'radicals' who had earned large fees on the college lecture circuit together with the organizational affiliation that established each man's radicalism by HISC criteria. Mr. Ciardi was cited for having supported The National Committee to Abolish the House Un-American Activities Committee."[49] Years before, in his Harvard days, Ciardi had been attacked in a somewhat similar way, the controversy not straying outside of Harvard-sponsored publications. Not only was Ciardi provoked to an impressive credo, but Cousins, now on his firmest ground, came to his defense in an editorial, " 'Radicals' and Mr. Ciardi." Aside from the irregularity, even the illegality, of the press release, the irate editor pointed out, Ciardi was not allowed to examine evidence against himself or granted any opportunity to make a statement. The story was widely covered "in all the news media." Cousins saw as a result that "colleges have now been provided with what in effect is a black list of speakers," to the possible impairment of the victims' incomes. Ciardi's congressman, Edward J. Patten, announced in the House that he had investigated the matter and found "not one single bit of evidence to justify Ciardi's name on the list." That statement appeared only in an inconspicuous item in the Perth Amboy (N.J.) *News/Tribune*, while "the original accusation was blared forth on television, radio, and the front page of newspapers." Cousins went on to bemoan that "equal time" was a "nicety reserved only for politicians engaged in political controversy," and that Congressman Patten was able to speak for only one man, whereas the others had no spokesmen,[50] which were perhaps his real points all along.

While the approximately 662,000 circulation of the *Saturday Review* may be tiny beside the audience reached by "all the news media," it is hardly an insignificant one, just as Norman Cousins is hardly an insignificant champion. Ciardi, however, was his own best spokesman in this matter. His "Manner of Speaking" essay of November 7, 1970, though it began "I am an ironist by profession," gave a forthright statement of his conception of his role as responsible citizen in the American democratic republic. He characterized himself as a "moderate liberal" and denied being at any time a radical, a radical being one who advocates the violent overthrow of the government. Any reader of Ciardi's columns would know him as too much a part of the well-to-do middle-class establishment for such radicalism, from which base, however, he insists on the right to unfettered use of his intellect and the responsible public disclosure of his findings. He did admit to opposing the methods of the House Un-American Activities Committee, predecessor of HISC, and earlier of the Dies Committee. Busy with his translation of Dante's *Paradiso*, he had not realized that HUAC had been succeeded by HISC. However, he took "all three of these committees to be sequentially one, and consistently in the pattern of McCarthyism." Since the charge against him was "reckless, cynical, or so seriously misinformed as to constitute an abuse of official responsibility," his point was well taken. He asked for a public apology from the HISC members, but did not get it. For all that Ciardi has been part of a powerful journalistic establishment, has been in his utterances a power himself, he stood up here for all responsible individuals against bigness and bullying. He had dedicated *Dialogue with an Audience* to Cousins "in that corner, wearing the purple trunks." In the terms of his own metaphor, he is also entitled to wear the purple trunks of the champion.

CHAPTER 2

The Early Poetry

I   *Hopwood Winner*—Homeward to America *(1940)*

IN this book Ciardi exhibits the first signs of many of his mature
characteristics. In that sense, the book is an organic part of his
work. Though he never reprinted poems from it, here is the real
beginning of his career as poet. The essential subject is a developing self in its relations to the modern world. Concomitantly, it
displays an irony which offers method, distance, attitude, tone.
Irony, which is so pervasive a quality in Ciardi's work, early and
late, that he can eventually speak of himself as an "ironist by
profession," is, in fact, almost an end in itself. Wit, too, is an
omnipresent quality, without which irony lacks grace and effectiveness. Because so many of the mature poet's qualities are
revealed here, if in inchoate form, the volume requires a scrutiny
not called for by its poetic merits alone.

   The book contains thirty-four poems, only three of them longer
than thirty lines. Thus Ciardi established at the beginning of his
career a preference for the short poem, a form which Yvor
Winters noted as the typical one of our time, capable of doing
anything we need done. The poems are grouped in four sections:
"Continent's Edge," "Latitudes and Longitudes," "City," and
"Suburbs." The first two are the best and seem to contain the
latest poetry; the others contain more of the experimental work
that never achieves consummation. Those in the fourth section in
particular seem to have little connection with their group title.
"Letters for the Next Time," with its 116 lines, is the most ambitious, but not the most successful. In more ways than not
Homeward to America is a book of the 1930s. The twenty-four-
year old poet had found a voice, voices rather, but few were entirely his own. The volume is a mixture of originality and
influences.

The title of the volume and the four titled sections suggest a journey coming to an end and a new beginning, in this case the journey of a young poet who has been on an intellectual grand tour. He may not like what he finds, but there is no choice but to return and confront the home conditions, which, of course, means also to confront his self. This theme is made clear in the first poem, "Letter to Mother," in which the poet sets up his own individuality as measure and subject in an adventure in the land new to his immigrant parents. Compressed into a few lines is a history of his family's experience, which he is to give in fuller detail for the rest of his career, adding new items each time. Just as the parents found their America "worth all / The coming," so the young poet must find his own: " . . . Mother, I can promise you nothing," for ". . . there will be no Americas discovered by analogy." Here is the fundamental commitment in Ciardi that caused Winfield Townley Scott to say, " . . . All of Ciardi's poetry is woven out of the belly of 'personal record.' "[1] The young poet's own journey is "across the sprung longitudes of the mind / And the blood's latitudes." As romantically, as vulnerably, but also as stubbornly as Bryon's Childe Harold he professes to "have made a sextant of heart / And nailed my bearings to sun. . . ." Still, "the hoped-for land" is not within hailing distance. Instead, the youth confronts "the enormous, wheeling, imperative sea," and "the high example" of his parents' immigration. To be true to them in the best sense, he must assert his independence.[2]

Two other poems, "Man Stranded" and "This Foolish Wing," offer possible answers to romantic quest. The first, a slight poem using sea and ship imagery, has a man left behind as his mates depart, despite his desperate efforts to rejoin them. In his plight, the man is forced to a final stand on his own nature, as, later, is the dying pilot from "Letter from a Rubber Raft" in *Live Another Day*. "This Foolish Wing," in two six-line stanzas, is more impressive. Using imagery from the romantic quests by flight to the ethereal regions, it poses another answer. The upper air cannot sustain such flights; wings tear, bodies sink to earth pointing "obvious and necessary truth," that "Time grows too late / For the torn ligament to attempt heaven." Romantic idealism was never attainable earlier and is even less possible now, what with the accumulated wounds suffered in earlier attempts; man simply cannot sustain the possibilities of his own intellectual conceptions.

More impressive than anything else about the poem is the skilled use of analogy to suggest the basic idea of accepting earthly limitations and making the most of them that is to be a recurrent note in Ciardi's work.

The most obvious weaknesses in the poems stem from their author's youth and inexperience, which have at their best the virtue of willful personalism. In "To One Investigated by the Last Senate Committee, or the Next," the fault stems from the fact that the actuality is not really within the young poet's experience; the result is an unconvincing abstraction. The poet is still a Prince Hal, not old enough to see the profundity of Falstaff. Years later, when Ciardi was cited as subversive by a congressional committee, he gives quite a different answer, one is certain, from what the youth, more his own man in intent than in fact, would have given.

"Visitor's Day at the Fort" is another fashionable exercise in which the values are more imagined than those which beat with the pulse of actual personal experience. The soldiers and their future deaths are seen as betrayed by commercial interests. Sinclair Lewis's George F. Babbitt is dragged inappropriately in as the epitome of hypocrisy that might shed a tear at the moving ceremony but still benefit financially from the soldiers' deaths. To its detriment the poem accepts too easily the leftist stereotypes and the rhetoric of the thirties.

Typical youthful values as youth sees itself are truth and courage, especially the courage to face the truth, as in "Night Lies." The Tennyson of "Ulysses" would have approved the general terms. If Ciardi had been doctrinairely religious, or if ours had been a religious age, this theme could have carried the name of "the fortunate fall." Instead, what comes out is a kind of secular humanism that better suits our modern age of unbelief, an age dominated by scientific materialism. For ideals, man must find within, himself become source and end, all the while granting his imperfectibility. This is essentially the mature Ciardi's position on that profoundest question of "What Is Man?"

"Having survived a theology and a war" goes a line in *Live Another Day*. The second is to come; if the first is done, it is just done, and the survivor is showing off his bravery and independence in his first book. The Eucharist is "the small diet of apostolic broth and the biscuits of a dead world" in "Letter to My Sisters at Home," and the speaker has "no answer made, knowing

no word / That will explain why love must work with poisons."
Mind is instructed in "The Night Lies" to "be shrewd, / Be cubic-
hard," presumably in order that those who grew up together
"may . . . advance now."

A pair of lines in "Anonymous" states, "The hardy heart must
come prepared / With more than love to travel long." Heart is
much present in the poems of section two, together with love, as
in "Boy with honor in your heart, / The world is not the world
you dream. . . ." Matthew Arnold had pointed this out in "Dover
Beach" for approximately the same reasons. What Ciardi said of
his friend Holmes's work in 1965 is true of his own youthful work:
"The word 'love' and the word 'heart' keep reappearing as
evidence that feeling had not yet burned through the easy
abstractions to reach the thing itself."[3]

One sees the youth in all of this more than anything else and is
persuaded of little else. In "To a Young American the Day After
the Fall of Barcelona," in a flash of rhetoric, we are given the
above honorable-hearted youth who "fed on the pure strain / Of
Aeschylean fire. . ." and had seen "Oedipus blinded, and the
sun / Gleaming on Promethean spleen, / And learned to love the
tragic day. . . ." This young literary man is urged to leave his
childhood and with the arms of "whetted wits and treach-
ery / And all resource of infamy. . ." go against the enemy in our
time, who is known to us, unlike the literary forces of the old
tragedies. As Ciardi was later to say, "Nothing is really hard but
to be real—" though at this time he might not have mocked the
phrase, because of the truth in it.

Another theme that shows up in *Homeward to America* and is
never to leave Ciardi's work is the definition of love. In "Letter to
J.R.R., the Last Transcendentalist," the situation seems to be an
exchange of letters between a pair of lovers; one (J.R.R.) has
urged the claims of transcendence for their love. Fortified by the
modern secularist faith in the unreality of universals, the narrator
replies. Though the ultimate literary source of this conflict may
be found in the great sonnet sequences like *Astrophel and Stella*,
and in Shakespeare's sonnet 128, and though some of Ciardi's best
lines (e.g., 22–27) echo Frost, the attitudes expressed are typical
of the young poet's work, and while they become richer and
deeper they remain prominent in his later work. In a sense, the
entire volume *I Marry You* (1958) is the mature poet's commentary on the young one's intentions. "A Conversation with Leon-

ardo" in *The Little That Is All* (1974) is a much later instance of
the abidingness of this conflict, there written even larger, between doubtful transcendence and human actuality.

In these young poems, Ciardi uses such devices as symbolic
landscapes ("Biography," "Cathedral," "Spring Song," "Letters
for the Next Time") and stereotypes ("Father Smith," "City");
both seem to come from literary idea and tradition as much as
from actual observation. The particulars are illustrations of ideas.
Soon he was to sharpen his skill so that at their best his particulars
seemed first themselves and after that symbols. His study of
Dante before the decade was out surely honed his sense of the particular that is itself and more—as much more as possible. The
result to come is a greater access of reality as the substantiality of
particulars becomes more convincing. Idea and image become
more nearly one.

Theme and tone may be the major accomplishments of
Homeward to America. The problems of belief, of definition, of
values (and of the self, too) are seen as acutely modern; therefore,
time is pertinent. Certain things from the past can no longer be
believed, but what is to replace them? Out of this dilemma
sounds the tone of uncertainty. As the earth moves into night, so
the human world also moves into a kind of night. Many of the images that carry the feelings have been forced or at least seem too
artificial to bear what the poet needs them to bear. Several poems
have weak endings ("City," "Homeward," "Spring"). The big effort, which is only intermittently successful, is to make what is
true for the young author (or what he thinks or wants to be true)
count as general truth. He is also unable to make what is intellectually fashionable count for him personally, though he tries. For
example, the social protest poems are the least effective. In this
relative failure lies the seed of the strongly individual poet that is
to come, when the protest arises from within him.

II   *The Stages to Maturity:* Other Skies *(1947) to* As If *(1955)*

Ciardi's next four books may be grouped together as showing
the stages in his maturing talent. Together they comprise some
200 poems, chosen from a much larger output. These volumes are
Other Skies (1947), *Live Another Day* (1949), *From Time to Time*
(1951), and *As If* (1955). The last is subtitled "Poems New and
Selected," and of its seventy-odd poems twenty-eight are from

three of the earlier collections. (Ciardi did not reprint any of the poems from *Homeward to America*.) The poet's talent was not in doubt in any of the volumes; what he would do with it, and what directions he was taking, were concerns of students of contemporary poetry, as both solicitous and scornful reviews indicated. But *As If* was a plateau of accomplishment on which the poet could take a proud stand. And from it the terrain ahead is discernible. It is reasonable for *I Marry You* (1958) to be grouped with these books because the poems are from the late war years forward rather than entirely new work.

III   Other Skies *(1947)*

War is the central experience of Ciardi's second volume, "by an accident of chaos," as he put it. There is the beginning, too, of that exploration and definition of the self that is to be his abiding subject. The book contains forty-two poems grouped into four sections to suggest scenes on the eve of the war, military training, air force combat in the Pacific, and impressions of postwar America. The first group has one poem only whose absence might be regretted, "Suddenly Where Squadrons Turn." In it, innocence and worldly wisdom are set in compassionate opposition. Skies are filled with squadrons of planes, while "In a green-tooled Paradise / The Innocent keep other skies. / We have much to learn." For example, if nature could achieve true harmony, then "Day would sing and love would thrive." The poem ends with an ironic rejoinder to Auden's "September 1, 1939": "Here across the iron sky / Iron squadrons simplify: / We must stay alive."[4] The other poems, merely witty, include a couple of beach scenes and a pair of poems from academic life, the first of a succession in Ciardi's work. Mostly, they are light verse in their presentation—playful, colloquial, irreverent—though the values expressed are serious enough. The theme of innocence versus experience looms up still but is treated with a wit more gay than grim. This also is to be a recurrent theme in the author's work. Early, the loss is regretted, while later its loss and the consequences are affirmed.

In these early poems, two things are worth noting. One, like an adolescent whose voice is changing, Ciardi is acquiring a recognizable voice of his own; and two, he writes in forms that, with variations, will continue into his other volumes. Ciardi uses

four-, five-, or six-line stanzas, the lines of varying metrical
length but symmetrical from stanza to stanza. The rhymes are
regular, though this poet likes to use stanzas without rhymes,
presumably held together by the rhythms rather than arbitrarily.
The run-on stanza appears frequently in *Other Skies* and gives
back some of the freedom that the strict stanzas would take away.
In such a way, Ciardi has found his balance between any needed
freedom and the demands of strict form. While ever a spokesman
for the freedom of a poet to pursue his own vision, he insists
equally, both in his prose and in his poetic practice, on the importance of form in poetry, extrinsic (stanza pattern, rhyme) and in-
trinsic (rhythm, repetitions, variations, and so on). Without this
control, communication is ineffective or impossible. Though he is
not beyond experiment and wide variations on conventional
forms, Ciardi has made such a conservative commitment in every
book he has written.

The other poems in the second book are ambitious in several
ways. Ciardi has a gift for aphorism and neat summary. As a sign
of greater complexity in these poems, however, the summary line
or couplet will not easily stand for the poem or its intention. The
interrelationships have been tightened; the whole is more complex, more organic. Another feature is the rather harsh contemporary imagery, sometimes developed in the manner of a modern
"metaphysical conceit." Aspects of the human are explored by the
metaphor of a machine in "First Summer After a War." This goes
naturally with the whole depersonalization that comes with
military life and war and which forces the troops into a detached
view of themselves, as in "Take-Off Over Kansas."

Ciardi's work is haunted by this military experience, which he
underwent in his late twenties. In the 1960s he recalled that he
had never given an order or taken one. The pose he presented in
Other Skies was the recalcitrant civilian looking at the folly about
him with amusement, wit, and sometimes compassion. By his
own evidence "Lucky John" had a "good war," but he has not
ceased to write against war as the ultimate obscenity or to ponder
the deaths he caused.

The popular touchstone for judging war poems seems to be the
verse of Wilfred Owen, ironic in the extreme but compassionate,
Randall Jarrell's hallucinated "Death of the Ball Turret Gunner,"
and perhaps Richard Eberhart's "The Fury of Aerial Bombard-
ment." Ciardi's best war poems are more comparable to the last.

The direct violent experience is kept in perspectives of reflection, reminiscence, and wit. In "Reflections While Oiling a Machine Gun," Ciardi thinks of Plato and how he had dismissed the philosopher as a spokesman to "the burgher," recalls a teacher "who loved George Washington and Hoover" and thought her young student a Communist because of his disrespect before her pieties. Seeing the ideals of a bourgeois society "which prefers its legend to its history" as having led to the war, he ends almost flippantly:

> Scholar in oil and steel and numbered parts,
> I have poor teacher's error at my thumb,
> And would request good voters of all sorts
> To lay less emphasis on Kingdom Come. (29)

This flippant, irreverent, socially critical attitude, with its tone to match, and its suggestions of middle-class error, would keep Ciardi's poetry from appealing to all but a few. The charge against it would be lack of sufficient seriousness. That is, we simply do not want wit and cleverness on some subjects, especially in wartime. This is a residue of the Puritanism that goes with what Ciardi is mocking.

"Death of a Bomber" is objective description and exposition seen by a collective "we" as part of which ". . . each man watched his own / Possible future flaming to arrive." The tone is appropriately solemn to the end, at which time ". . . when we left the last fire and last smoke / Someone began a drawn-out bedroom joke." In "Saipan," also with the collective "we" as narrator, the men are abashed that once it seemed clouds and winds and weathers had loved them, while now, as airmen, they are part of the sweeping weather that leaves dead in their wake.

Another poem impersonal in its method is "Elegy" ("For Kurt Porjescz, Missing in Action, 1 April 1945"). It achieves a dignity, a lyric intensity, and a developed metaphor that are admirable:

> The boys are flowers: they strew themselves in seed
> And spring again, anonymous and pure,
> For the same tears to follow the same deed
> Of bending in the wind, and soon and sure
> Fold, fall, and fade from what they could not cure.

. . . .

April is their return in chlorophyl.
Protein and water celebrate their root.
The lavish world's extravagance, they till
The loamy crust, while blindly underfoot
They crush their own unrecognized green shoot. (51)

The airmen (boys, really, for they are "like boys gone to school wearing their badges") become part of the recurrence of spring in a way other than their youth as a result of their "last high passage and . . . faltering luck."

Ciardi's tone, his own, is in this poem appropriately elegiac. The elegy is emotional, lyrical. Ciardi's poems are as strongly emotional as those of any modern poet; at the same time, intellect is also pronounced. Doubtless the two are often in conflict, but at his most successful, in a given poem, the two function smoothly together to produce an example of unified sensibility. Emotion and intellect in creative tension become a unity. Though this union may be achieved only sporadically in separate poems, it is sufficient.

Ciardi's poems could be charged, as were those of the Metaphysicals by Dr. Johnson, with "the most heterogeneous ideas . . . yoked by violence together." T. S. Eliot clarified, "The force of this impeachment lies in the failure of the conjunction, the fact that often the ideas are yoked but not united. . ." and added that "a degree of heterogeneity of material compelled into unity by the operation of the poet's mind is omnipresent in poetry."[5] In fact, much of what Eliot says in his 1921 justification of the Metaphysical poets also applies to Ciardi as well. He is one of the company of modern poets (Eliot was talking about Jonson and Chapman) who are "notably erudite, and . . . who incorporated their erudition into their sensibility; their mode of feeling was directly and freshly altered by their reading and thought . . ." including "a direct sensuous apprehension of thought, or a recreation of thought into feeling. . . ." Surely, even at this early stage, we can see that Ciardi (again in Eliot's words for seventeenth-century poets) has in large measure "a mechanism of sensibility which could devour any kind of experience." And he too may be "simple, artificial, difficult, or fantastic."[6] This use of Eliot's words implies nothing of magnitude in the comparison. Ciardi has not undone Donne or Dante (in whose work these qualities also pertain). The cousinship may be remote and Ciardi's successes rare, but the similitude is real.

The best-known poem from *Other Skies* is "Elegy Just in Case," on the author himself imagined as a casualty. In it appears another example of wit that seems more characteristic of the seventeenth century than of the twentieth, one that is both light and serious at the same time. The poem has been held in special esteem by its author, for in 1964 he mentioned the many revisions he had put the poem through in an effort to explore and capture the possibilities of its theme. Jonathan Swift's elegy on himself was part of its inspiration, Ciardi admitted.[7]

It takes a special kind of sensibility to be humorous over the prospect of one's own death rather than morbid and self-pitying:

> Here lie Ciardi's pearly bones
> In their ripe organic mess.
> Jungle blown, his chromosomes
> Breed to a new address. (45)

The poem ends with several stanzas on the haunting memory of a sexual experience:

> Darling, darling, just in case
> Rivets fail or engines burn,
> I forget the time and place
> But your flesh was sweet to learn. (46)

Though Ciardi admitted that sex was one of the great experiences for him,[8] the theme of sex in his poems becomes greater after his marriage. If there is no core of profundity or belief in this poem, there is still the ironic attitude and the bravado in the face of death.

Ciardi's war poems have not been given their due in collections and writings on the subject. One would surmise that his wit would have been taken as frivolity, his mockery of officialdom as lack of patriotism, his irony as cynicism. With two unwon wars between us and *Other Skies*, Ciardi's poems seem authentic responses in their lack of a preponderant tone of high seriousness. More important than that is what is shown about Ciardi's development. With the first volume behind him, he could concentrate on finding his own voice—and that may be the real accomplishment of this second volume, that voice, slangy yet learned, irreverent yet concerned, pious before his own holiness but not beyond self-mockery, in short the American wiseguy with

a heart, this one articulate and ambitious and intent upon
capitalizing on both qualities.

The same capacity to see himself in perspective—a tendency to
become a pronounced and fixed part of Ciardi's work—appears
in "On a Photo of Sgt. Ciardi a Year Later." Presumably, the
picture was made during the war and observed from the vantage
of a year's time. About illusion and reality, done flippantly and so
about innocence and knowledge, the poem states that "The
camera always lies. By a law of perception / The obvious surface
is always an optical ruse." Recognizing "The careful slouch and
dangling cigarette" as self-conscious poses, the poet is aware too
that "The shadow under the shadow is never caught: / The
camera photographs the cameraman."

Suppose that Ciardi had not undergone the military experience. The war would have been distant in the poems; there would
have been sugar and shoe and gas rationing, manless classes and
man-hungry girls, and so on. This is only to note that, for all of
the grim details of war, Ciardi is more interested in his own
responses and experiences than in the war itself. He is on the way
to his not yet fully discovered true subject—himself. The perspectives of these two Sgt. Ciardi poems seem important steps in the
emergence of his major theme.

Related also to the Sgt. Ciardi poems are four birthday poems
in *Other Skies*. Perhaps following Dylan Thomas's "Twenty-four
Years" and later birthday poems, Ciardi has "Night Piece for My
Twenty-seventh Birthday," "Reveille for My Twenty-eighth
Birthday," "Poem for My Twenty-ninth Birthday," and "Poem
for My Thirtieth Birthday"; in later volumes he adds "Poem for
My Thirty-second Birthday" in *Live Another Day* and "Poem for
My Thirty-ninth Birthday" in *As If*.

"Night Piece" is a lost-innocence poem, too cryptic, too com-
pacted for certain of its references to be entirely clear, though the
irony of a universe in which the laws of nature and the laws of
man, especially man at war, seem to be the same is the tension of
the poem.

In "Reveille," the young airman, aged twenty-eight, is routed
from an erotic dream only to be "ranked and numbered in my
morning place" in which everything is seemingly ordered, all
questions answered: "Law shall keep me, and Command provide. . . ." The conflict between the human reality and the
military codification of the no longer human creature is the basis

of the poem. The metaphor of man as machine is developed until

> I am the theorem of the pure believer:
> The thumbs for switches and the hands for pliers
> Moved on a diagram of nerves like wires. (25)

Abashed to find himself "Journeyman expert in the trades of kill, / Scholar of bomb and fuse . . ." his hand having become "a stranger's claw," he hopes that "Time may return it," but in the meantime his training in the military skills must dominate. The closest thing to the grand sentiments of Rupert Brooke is here in what may be self-pity masking as ironic grimness:

> . . . and though the mountain burn
> I am the bachelor of three schools of law
> And have my trade, precise and equally:
> To burn by air, to shoot by land, to drown by sea. (27)

Using a day's bombing mission from Saipan to Japan as the pattern, Ciardi achieves a new intensity of irony and compassion, the latter as much for the bombers as the bombed, in "Poem for My Twenty-ninth Birthday." It is addressed to "gentle stay-at-home," and the airman is signing "in fire your and my heritage: / The bomb whose metal carcass dressed and bled / Is our day's gift to populate the dead." The terrible ambiguity of the mechanized war against an unseen and unhated enemy is indicated as "Our bombs descend to save or kill us all." Now part of inhuman mechanization, the airmen see their results in natural metaphors: "(We fire at fighters and await the rose / Blossoming in fire upon the town / Whose living history we have come to close.)" And the remote, impersonal quality of the experience: "The dead are not our loss. My memory is / Our simplest day was guiltier than this." What is the result? The young smart aleck is no more, at least for the time being. This man, "blossomed awkwardly from dragon seed," has gone deep into the unresolvable, beyond "You, endlessly the pure and gentle heart." Death has cast shadows "On all the reasoned motions of the mind." Though Ciardi is ever to stress that poems have their valid truths without the necessity of being true to biographical or other fact, one is certain that this poem is true in both ways. One is equally certain this man will never be quite the same again.

The war as the ultimate stupidity was never to leave Ciardi's imagination, though he realized its continual likelihood as an immemorial course of human action, to be expected, given man's nature. Ciardi was less interested in the immediate causes than in the experience of war, both on the emotions and nerves, and in what the mind makes of it upon reflection. Close to the experience, he saw V-J Day in a poem of that title as "the tallest day in time" in which "the dead came back" in a vision of those who did not survive, but were part of the terrible cost of the war. For all the survivors' delight in their own fortune, still "all the dead were homing": "On the tallest day in time we saw them coming / Wheels up and flaming on a metal sea."

The poet who stayed alive is still haunted in "First Summer After a War" by the unreason of war. This poem gives signs of the change away from the fashionable, somewhat sentimental humanism of *Homeward to America* toward the bleaker view in which man is imaged as a machine or as something nature makes use of in its slow processes. What else is one to make of those who "died in a cliché of history"?

> Their hands like gauges, their eyes like screens
>   To signal and record electric djinns,
> Their skulls like batteries, their wired veins,
>   And the brittle insulation of their skins. (70)

The above lines may show the influence or at least the inspiration of Donne. Also, there are echoes of Auden: "Compassion is the orator's easiest fraud, / And sorrow a public camouflage . . ." and of Yeats: "Nothing is born to sing but what its birth / Is swaddled in political distress." Death is also machinelike, is compared to bulldozers which cover the trenches filled with the dead. All that comes of the piled dead for civilization is the poet's response with their elegy. Man is under sentence of death anyway, and death as bulldozer is no more grotesque than the rest of the consequences of war. For purposes of civilization and all meaning that is possible to human life, man must "Live in the waking center of his dream . . ." or else death the machine, "Whose tread is on the furrows of the dead, / Whose living fuel we are . . ." prevails. We bring it inevitably about "once we have forfeited / Our civil dream and waking discontent." In other words, man has a chance to create himself. This poem picks up ideas from *Homeward to America* on the failure of nerve and will and gives them a much better, that is, a subtler, profounder, and more convincing statement. He is near to the discovery of his great subject—himself. From Voltaire's Candide on, that has been garden enough to cultivate, and from the Romantics, continent enough to explore.

Near the end of *Other Skies*, "Poem for My Thirtieth Birthday" (June 24, 1946) combines most of the qualities of the book. Soon, the poet is to be married. It is a love poem, a war poem, an epithalamium, and an elegy. Waking to a new day, at the beginning of a new life, the poet cannot get out of his mind the recent military experiences with death. Time has him under a death sentence that could be mitigated by the simple religion of his childhood, no longer available:

> And still the wish is theological:
> Though saints are out of office and heaven not listed,
> Our hungry cells, whose motive is groceries,
> Are speculative fools and have invested
> In heavens of their own. They plan on margin
> And fail at last, but for a while they win. (82)

The poem is full of the contemporary references and images that will prevail in Ciardi's poems. Also, Ciardi, bound increasingly to truthfulness in regard to his own experience, seems to have difficulty in ending a poem. Miller Williams and others have said he goes too far and throws effects away, ruins a poem by telling too much, narrowing down the possibilities by the aphoristic tendency. This is something to notice throughout Ciardi's work. There is some truth to the charge. The two explanations that have been suggested are honesty and aphoristic ability. Perhaps back of everything is a desire for significance coupled with a kind of pedagogical intent, to make his own experience count for the mind as well as to count for the mind of a reader. One would suspect as much from the next volume, *Live Another Day*, which opens with a provisional statement of his principles in prose.

IV   Live Another Day *(1949)*

It is difficult for a critic to resist saying that a new note in a poet's work is a development in the man. With Ciardi, the new note or notes in *Live Another Day* were not entirely new themes or experiences. The poems do seem more solidly his own even when less personal. He tried to present a few experiences that are not his own except by imagination. Related to these things, at least, is a new concern for the state of the world and of the nature and quality of life in general, as opposed to any youthful idealism, and thus a new maturity. Diminished are the flippancy and easy irony at the expense of the world and life's small situations, even if these were extrapolated into larger significance. For purposes of the poetry, there does appear to have been a real growth in Ciardi's humanity, mind, and heart. He was married by this time, and that was important to him—how important will culminate in *I Marry You*. In the first two volumes he took the smaller situation and wrote it large; in the third volume he seems to have had the larger vision and concerns and to dramatize them by means of particular, smaller, often personal situations. He appears to have made a determined effort at breaking out of any exclusively personal subjectivity, so that in these poems he seeks new possibilities for depth, breadth, and resonance unrealized in most of the earlier ones. The pitfalls may be greater—preaching, propaganda, abstraction, insincerity, failure to find an adequate vehicle to express the idea, or a failure to feel sufficiently what the mind perceives (especially important in that Ciardi, for all of his excellent mind and his brilliant wit, was and is very much the man of feeling). Though he carries on here the imagery of man as machine and man as so much meat or protein in nature—these as part of his vision of man without immortal soul and without God—the new concern is for the values of civilization, considered positively, values for a man to live by. This new emphasis may be played off against the irony of earlier poems at the triviality of things to die for, and not just triviality, but also ridiculousness and grotesqueness. The personal is not eschewed entirely in this quest for new values in that personal responsibility, freely and rationally chosen, is preeminent. For the poet, art is his personal answer, but art seen as inseparable from civilization, actually held more as a faith than proved. Though this attitude is true of such older poets as Eliot and Pound, Ciardi cites their poems as instances of private (which is not identical with personal) aestheticism and, therefore, as not socially responsible. In these poems, Ciardi showed that he can get free of all kinds of things, such as religion, family, and childhood, for purposes of his art; but he cannot get rid of his memory or his experiences, those things which are himself. His problem as an artist may be seen as the difficulty of reconciling these two strains in his work, the personal and the public, with the added need to speak in a unique voice that is also his own, whatever the synthesis that results.

The first sign of Ciardi's relatively more public concern in *Live Another Day* is the six-page "Foreword to the Reader of (Some) General Culture." This hypothetical reader expanded to the collective is the same one with whom Ciardi would hold his "dialogue with an audience" in his first collection of essays. His specifications are:

> He goes to symphony. He likes to spend an afternoon at the museums and galleries and he has some notion of what he looks at there. He knows part of the difference between the Ballet Russe and a chorus-line. He has read enough psychology to know that only an expert should tamper with Freud. He is aware that ideas have histories, and that the ideas held by the people about him are usually retrograde in the best history of things. He has browsed through philosophy in a general way. He knows that other societies have come before his and others will come after his and that none have been absolute and that none will be, but that some common dynamics of the human spirit has shown through them all, and that the best name anyone has found to give to that dynamics is Art. . . .
>
> Or he is, if you prefer, a man at least as well educated as the poet (usually no incredible feat), but not in a literary specialty. I mean to stress the word "educated" and I mean it to exclude the technicians. Technicians are not educated; they are trained. Education does not occur except where questions of human value are invoked. . . . We must learn to value only the civilized man.[9]

Ciardi suspects that in the long run this type is more important for poetry than Eliot and Pound are.

By and large, these qualities would seem to be projections of a well-to-do middle-class conception of all in modesty it can aspire to produce in the way of a man of culture. The description fits very well Henry James's young women, on whom he supposed the future of America to depend. One aspect of this address is Ciardi's fighting clear of Eliot and Pound's influence on modern letters. Ciardi saw them as specialists writing for specialists; they are in his denomination (borrowed from Antonio Machado as translated by H. L. Davis) "baroque poets," by which Ciardi means no more than that their writing "addresses itself inward to other writing, rather than outward to the lives of men." Possibly he is even more under the influence of MacLeish's *The Irresponsibles*, or just the general Northeastern Liberalism to which Ciardi has basically always subscribed (though as he became more affluent and settled, he cleaved to different parts of it). However much his views of Eliot and Pound may be disputed (and he throws in Robert Graves for good measure), Ciardi was joining many young poets—Viereck, Shapiro, Lowell, and Jarrell for example—at this time in speaking up for greater communicability, greater rapprochement with a wider audience. They sought not to debase poetry or truckle to any audience; they would be modern, they would be difficult, even obscure, but simply not so private as to be inaccessible to a reader who would take the trouble to work a bit.

As part of Ciardi's *ars poetica*, he lists thirteen principles, intended not for critics but for his general readers as "a basic simplification of the general outlook and techniques from which he tried to write poems." He further characterized them as "a reassertion of . . . sound and enduring principles and practices . . ." which can "offer a hope and future for poetry" in saving it from the Baroque.

These thirteen aspects of what he considered the true tradition are: "A poem should be understandable"; "Poetry should be read aloud"; "Poetry should be about the lives of people"; "Poetry should be specific"; "There is no subject not fit for poetry and no word not fit for poetry"; "Art from which no personality emerges is dead"; "In a successful poem the subject must create its own form"; "Whenever a poem seems to be saying two things at once, it is saying two things at once, and should be so understood"; "There is no such thing as a poem that does not affirm"; "A line of poetry is a conceived unit, not a typographical fragment"; "A poem is not a syllogism, and its essential unity and progression are psychological rather than logical"; "Rhyme (internal as well as line-end) is not an appliqued ornamentation, but part of the total voice-punctuation of the poem"; "The norm of English metrics is the iambic pentameter line, but the best poetry is written less out of a strict observance of that line, than out of a sensitively trained memory of it with wide variations in the number of light beats in a foot." Some of these are expounded and illustrated, some are not. Reviewers jumped on this or that or another point, one thinking Ciardi claimed that he tested everything he wrote by these principles before he put it down on paper, another finding the brief essay on metrics to be nonsense. Ciardi thought well enough of this essay to reprint it in *Mid-Century American Poets* as his statement about poetry. All he had claimed was that he wrote out of a general background of these beliefs. Many of the principles enunciated are part of the general modern approach to poetry, coming from the New Critics and others. Ciardi is of course eclectic, but there is no reason to question that he held to these principles as values in poetry, including his own. How far he could go beyond them while not repudiating them is shown in *How Does a Poem Mean?* These statements, like everything Ciardi has done, are the work of a practicing poet.

There are several notable achievements in *Live Another Day*, some to be pursued and developed in later volumes, others to remain as solitary landmarks of what Ciardi could do. The epigraph for one of the groups of poems is "Intellectual pessimism, but glandular enthusiasm." Though this sentiment would need to be qualified at length before it could stand as generally true of Ciardi's verse, nevertheless the creative tension between the two tendencies establishes the boundaries of his work. Another instance of an attitude that recurs throughout his work is the epigraph for still another group of poems. "We never knew such palms as these," a marveling voice says. But "the monkey of these trees / Flashes his pink indecencies, / Chatters irate obscenities," and prevents sleep by hurling cocoanuts at the, perhaps, expended lovers. "Put on your clothes," the voice says, "There is no Eden, no repose. / Back to the ice where we were born / The other side of Capricorn." If the pessimism appears to dominate right now, the eventual reconciliation is to affirm what has been gained despite the cost, "the little that is all." Here, nonetheless, is a sign of a doubleness that riddles Ciardi's work from early to late.

The concern for civilization appears in "Stone Works," an image which is used several times in Ciardi's work and represents approximately the fundamentals from which structures may be built. In this poem the past is lost as in the culture of the Easter Island stone heads, or bad as in the Norfolk Island stone gallows from which prisoners were strangled with slow nooses, or decayed as on Bougainville and Saipan where sculptures slowly rot in the jungle. The latter are a backdrop for the "Shock of arrival of / A manchild serialized to eight digits," surely dogtagged airman Ciardi himself, who in this and other poems imagined himself as a corpse consigned to such natural agencies. That was "the worst," and he had survived it. To what end was the slow progress: "The manchild / In a museum of corpses . . . / Inches on his stomach / To a minimum altitude, / And is all of us"? Having learned in his jungle that "The trick is / Not to die / A little longer," he brought his small redemption of knowledge to us.

Another poem that in its time might have passed for a war poem because of its imagery is "Letter from a Rubber Raft." A phrase from this poem gives *Live Another Day* its title. In relatively free form, the poem depicts the desperation of a downed pilot afloat on a liferaft. He speaks on the twelfth, thirteenth, fourteenth, and eighteenth days, then later asks, "*Which day is this?*" and, near his end, simply denominates the time as "Later." He is the sole survivor of eleven men, undone because someone gave them dirty gasoline by mistake. The military paraphernalia is of no significance in the poem except, perhaps, that we have modern technological man, who has certain expectations, confronting the ultimate. It is hardly necessary for the reader, but to the dying pilot on the fourteenth day of his ordeal comes the revelation that he is a symbol for Man in the universe. He thinks of his late comrades, of love, of the one fish he caught, and makes crude verse of fish, God, sea, love, and death. The mixture of hope and dogged determination with resignation comes out in the last lines:

> It is not hard to let go. I cannot.
> I have eaten all my bait but my line is out:
> If some foolish fish will bite metal
> I may live another day. (40)

The poem is far from an entire success in any of its aspects. Yet here, once again, is "man alone" with his subjectivity and the immensity of an alien universe. He has his memories of the best which life had offered him, he has a feeble creativity, but life on any terms that will allow survival is the immediate requirement, and that is not met. Ultimately, the strength of the poem, imperfectly realized, comes from the fact that it is a parable of diminishment, an analogue for all of life. As such, it might be grouped with "History is What a Man Does" in *The Little That Is All* and with many others. Yet, on the other side, as Ciardi said in

"Philosophical Poem," "Above all, I have no case against human nature. / Whatever that is, I like it."

One aspect of human nature is explored in *Live Another Day* in seven poems collected under the title "Summer in Missouri" with the following epigraph:

> They have an answer to their lives,
> Have learned to take what the land gives,
> Admire their kind, and always vote.
> They work harder than the hired hand.
> All that a man can learn by rote
> From five to nine, they understand. (65)

The summer was evidently spent with his in-laws in rural eastern Missouri. The poems include the Northeastern liberal's concern for civilization because country children with their .22 caliber rifles learn violence and killing, from which trivial practice great wars may eventuate. This view does not look very deeply into one's own heart in these mostly personal poems. They record a kind of failure. Nothing he knew was "native to this place," certainly not himself. He wondered what to do, aware that "This is as far as I shall ever go / Out of the world, uneasy to return" ("Letter from a Metaphysical Countryside"). Ciardi failed to respond with one of the perennial and immemorial human impulses of finding peace, God, aspects of the self in nature. He more nearly learned what William Carlos Williams had said in "Raleigh Was Right," that "We cannot go to the country / for the country will bring us no peace." Ciardi was bored and lacked his often brash confidence, as he stood in irony amidst the alien corn, a city boy confronted with an uncongenial culture. His powers of empathy—never his strong point—simply did not extend this far; but if nothing else he learned for certain something he was not, could not, or did not want to be. His sense of frustration invites the reader's sympathy.

Possibly the best of the country poems is the unpretentious "Survival in Missouri," one that Ciardi reprinted in *As If*. He is nearly always good when drawing from his childhood. Here he recalled how he had "thought too much" about the death during childhood of a friend, Willie Crosby, a subject he took up again in two notable poems, "Mystic River" in *From Time to Time* and "Two Saints" in *Lives of X*, with a different emotional emphasis

each time. Relatives and the Irish priest marvelled over his boyish
grief:

> . . . . *Such sorrow.*
> *He really lived in that boy.*
> *Here now, you gowonoff to the movies.*
> *Give your grief to God.* (69)

These, the responses respectively of "Sister and Mother and Uncle
and Father O'Brien. . . ." Ironically, he went to both the movies
and the "lovely wake" at which everyone admired him for his
grief. Now twenty years later in Missouri, a crop-drowning rain is
as unwanted a gratuity as Willie's death. And the bitter knowledge: "Having survived a theology and a war, / I am beginning
to understand / The rain." There was no habitation for the big
city boy in nature; it was no more friendly than death.

Two other poems in the book deserve mention. Both are longer
at 157 and 149 lines than most of the early poems. One, "Letter to
Virginia Johnson," is a qualified success; the other, "A Guide to
Poetry," perhaps influenced by Karl Shapiro's "Essay on Rime,"
is a witty failure. The eponymous lady of the former appears to be
a psychiatrist. The poem itself is Ciardi's "Essay on Man." It is
the closest thing to an explicit statement of his ideas on the nature
of man he has given in his poems. Intellect dominates the poem,
and the language is abstract. It has thirteen stanzas which range
in length from eight to sixteen lines. The epigraph gives the key-
note to the ideas and the values. We will not achieve to the
measure of our belief, or escape from unconscious forces; nevertheless, "Let us at least admire sanity / With all possible conviction and a touch of urbanity." "Our Times" define man in a
"scholastic tongue," the language of science. Whether modern
men are "ascending or descending" by comparison to earlier, we
must "begin / A recognition of necessity." It is man's nature to
seek for ultimate purpose; in this, man has always been the same,
even if he "Changes his vision with every change of dress." We
must, as Matthew Arnold has said, see him steadily and see him
whole, which means to accept his essential nature under his varying garb. Man is unique in the evolutionary scale; no other
creature is a measure for him. The "measure of man's improving
sight" shall instead be those who accept the partial emancipation
from legend to the necessity for change, and those like Virginia

herself who treat the modern mind's ailments. "Our Times" have ended the age of Faith and begun the "Age of Evidence," because science has disproved religion; on his own, man is "prodigy enough / To be the measure of his own intent. . . ." Primitive man created God to explain phenomena, but nineteenth-century science changed all that forever. "The starry outline of a father face" that earlier man thought he had seen in the sky has receded beyond the reach of telescopes; the sky is silent, empty. It is up to man to come "to a final recognition," that he is a doomed creature subject to impulse, chance, and circumstance "with neither freedom nor integrity," unless this lead him to self-efforts, and finally to make a "studious decision" to become "the mechanic of revision." That is grim but far from hopeless. There is a forthright manliness about it. A still-young poet could live by it; he could even expect his beloved new wife to live, not too uncomfortably, by it. One is entitled to doubt it could remain unaltered once the children started to come.

The "Guide to Poetry" is a satiric guide to "making it" in contemporary poetry. It was dedicated to "Cid Corman, who needs it least." It is narrow in its pertinence and in its references. Wit is its chief quality. Implicit is Ciardi's pride in his own commonsense, working-poet's approach to art. It makes fun of certain tendencies that seemed more true in the forties than since. He showed a good understanding of the preciosity academic and literary coteries fall into easily, and a fine contempt for both. He handled imaginary dialogue well. An individual going his own way and proud of his own accomplishment wrote this barbed epistle in rhymed couplets and triplets. One clever passage contains five lines of the actual critical jargon (*"Presyllabic vowel, magnetic tension, / Caudate syntax, consonantal flexion,"* etc.) worked into the metrical and rhyme pattern of his text. Very likely at this time he did not foresee that in ten years he would be subject to similar objections because of the terminology he made up for *How Does a Poem Mean?* Luckily, there was no real meanness in the "Guide to Poetry," but only good-humored contempt. Like Byron with "English Bards and Scotch Reviewers," Ciardi did not repeat this performance. He could do it if he wanted to, so why bother. The impulse to light verse with its pronounced rhymes more nearly spilled over into the children's verse where it could be as violent as the author pleased without danger of being taken too seriously.

V   From Time to Time *(1951)*

Despite several excellent poems that are as good as anything he had written up to this time, *From Time to Time* is not on the whole an appealing volume. Of its forty-four poems, many seem experimental, as though the poet were forcing himself to branch out in new directions that turned out not really to be his own. The experiments, if that is what they are, were not always successful, at least they are not the things one thinks of as the essential Ciardi. Conceivably the book could be regarded as transitional, but since specific words, images, and ideas do not recur with any frequency in the author's later work, we may take this fact as a sign they are in fact experimental, Ciardi looking for himself in verse. The poems showed a new influence from Wallace Stevens. The result was that many poems were highly abstract and intellectual. Little enough passion and emotion were here, and without them the Ciardi we think we know at any stage of his career disappears. The poems have much wit and many grotesque conceits and strange fantasies. One can more nearly respect them than feel or like them. Too, one can easily suspect many of the poems to be forced or contrived. By the most uncharitable extension of this allegation of motive, one wonders if by such means the poems seek to avoid triteness and sentimentality. The author himself thought well enough of the poems to reprint eighteen of them in *As If.* For that matter, no book could be an entire loss that contained "Mystic River," "The Evil Eye," and "Childe Horvald to the Dark Tower Came." After that, one has several choices. One other positive feature of the book is that here Ciardi begins the exploration of his Italian identity that is to be one of his most fruitful themes. The poems on his father, his mother, and his various relatives come under this category, as does the entire volume *Lives of X.* Here, too, is the first concern with his name as an analogue of his identity. We know the concern Dante's characters have for their names and everything touching the names. In his notes to the *Inferno* Ciardi tells how this is still a concern in modern Italy.[10] Whether acquired or natural, it is certainly true for him.

Let us begin with the negative, the Wallace Stevens resemblance, for it is here the abstractions are most evident. Influences are very difficult to show, and the profounder ones may not show at all. Every writer borrows from, responds to, is influenced by

any number of other writers and thinkers. This is no doubt as it
should be. The influences that are easily perceivable are the
superficial ones. So it is with Ciardi and Wallace Stevens. A few
phrases, an idea or two that would be more at home in the work
of the older poet—it amounts to not much more than that. Ciardi
could have been drawn to the work of Stevens for any number of
reasons. Both have secular visions of life, and both value the
imagination as a great force in life. Stevens found a method and a
language in which to embody such a vision and such values. Seeing things that were similar to his own, Ciardi tried the letter of
them for himself. Would the man of (some) general culture question if told the following lines came from Stevens?

> Song, song,
> So-ong, the crickets. And *blop, blop, b-lop*
> The frogs. And *ago, ago, ago*
> Says the rational man in the shadow. (This is his sop
> To the passionate man in the song.)[11]

Present are Steven's playful fondness for sounds, his juxtaposition
of "sop" with "rational" and "passionate" men considered as
abstractions.

In other poems, Stevens-like qualities appear, such as a rhetorical posing as other characters for the sake of argument, the use of
unrhymed couplets and triplets, and especially the examination
of various degrees of reality, such as the reality of supposing. The
qualities here would be more influenced by *Parts of a World* and
Transport to Summer than *Harmonium*. Anybody could write a
poem entitled "Man in Bed with Asthma," but in the present
context, when Ciardi does, it sounds like Stevens. The five-part
poem "The Extraction of Concept from Nature" has as its section
titles the following: "A Day in Three Families," "Of Coloration as
a Legality," "Metaphor as Concept," "*Con templus* as a root in
Augury (a note on III.)," and a "A Footnote on Metaphor as
Environment," and a number of Stevens-like lines. One merely
observes here that Ciardi is better when a poem does not require
him to be too clever, but to stick to his own kind of irony and his
ever-reliable feelings. His own sensibility gives his best results.

Other echoes of Stevens appear in "The Cartographer of
Meadows," which begins:

> The cartographer of meadows does not rose
> His meridians. There is no north in a bramble.
> Nor south nor anywhere in a scroll of thorns
> In blue grass. They are simply consecutive with.
> As the bee is born knowing the trumpet flower
> Is at once everywhere he comes upon it. (49)

The problem is not that Ciardi is not entitled to explore any of these things. Philosophical considerations crop up in his work all the way through. And thematically, even here, the poem, in its concern for the proper use of human beings as opposed to the wartime use, is closer to Ciardi than to Stevens. If the experiments with Stevens's manner in any way helped him to the achievement of "Thoughts on Looking into a Thicket" from *As If*, in which he is every bit as philosophical as the older poet but in no way resembles him in concept or manner, then all such "influences" are justified.

From Time to Time begins with a "Foreword," which is a poem entitled "The Figure I Drawn in Wire," with the "I" written by hand to resemble an inverted fishhook. If the poem is not entirely successful, it nonetheless brings out the humanistic idea pervasive in his later work that each man by being himself is every man, is all men. The poem is a kind of "song of myself" in thirty-two lines. An epigraph from the English poet Roy Fuller continues the note of social responsibility stated at length in *Live Another Day*: "art has duties to— / As well as to the 'I'—the 'You.'" In the poem, "the Curlicue Ego" is posed in its crooked ways as "A tangle, a small snare, or a fishhook." The three categories above are developed in a five-line stanza each. The developments are clever, but for a thematic examination of Ciardi's poems the conclusion is the most important. Whatever is caught from within by whatever kind of hook or trap, the result is "The all-in-all, the me in you, the you in me." To get a really notable poem from the application of this article of faith, Ciardi needed the emphasis on his Italian identity and other personal particulars, but from the general concept he never swerved.

A poem that shows how Ciardi can draw from intensely personal material in his own background and yet generalize the meaning is "Mystic River," one of his best poems, entirely in his own voice and manner. Much more straightforward than some other poems in *From Time to Time*, it does not seem forced, but natural, something actually experienced and then realized as a poem. Ciardi's river runs through Medford, Massachusetts; his childhood was spent on its banks. These aspects are presented in detail in "The River" in *Lives of X*, in which he explores the New England background at its point of intersection with the Italian immigrants of whom Ciardi was the son. But in "Mystic River" the past is juxtaposed to his own childhood, the nature of which is unspecified except as to its idyllic if mutable qualities. Seeing the river recover "The first sweet moon of time tonight," he quotes the words of "the Gods" (the early settlers). Their acquisitiveness has led to a "Civilization of silt and sewerage." The poem is notable for its suggestibility, as in "Their land / Is an old land where nothing's planted / Beside the rollerdrome and hot dog stand. . . ." Even if the "Gods" are dead, their results accrue still. Of the years between the Edenic vision of the first settlers and present pollution, the poet has "stoned and swum and sculled them all." The course of the river in time parallels the development of America on the one hand and the course of American innocence to present awareness in his own person. This theme is reinforced by details from his own experience and the juxtapositions of these with the earlier references. There is no "inconsistence of sensibility," as a reviewer had charged;[12] for the details, ugly as they intentionally are, carry the theme:

> Naked behind the birches at the cove
> Where Winthrop built a landing and a yawl
> And tabloids found a famous corpse of love
> Hacked small and parceled into butcher's paper,
> Joe La Conti stumbled on an old pauper
>
> Dying of epilepsy or DT's,
> And I came running naked to watch the fit.
> We had to dress to run for the police. (20)

Ciardi was honest enough to wonder whether they had "run for help or the joy of it." From the same river, Willie Crosby of "Survival in Missouri" and "Two Saints" (*Lives of X*) had caught a fever and died. In "Mystic River" this death followed the ugly growth of a civilization from which "Our naked bank bled broken tiles and nails." These things lend a poignance to the lines that are almost more wondering than grim: "So I know death is a dirty river / At the edge of history. . . ." Technically, Ciardi has become a master of controlling the tone of his more successful poems. Under the spell of the moonlight on the river, the poet bursts forth with "Oh rotten time, rot from my mind to night!" Momentarily, he almost wants the illusion to be all. The last two stanzas show many of Ciardi's qualities, first technically in their repetition and variation and suggestiveness: light is the moon's illusion that gives way to dawn; it is also the light of knowledge that cannot be removed though it can have many positive results; and, thematically, it expresses an affirmation despite all reasons to the contrary:

> Let me be richly lit in this one stir,
> And where the Gods grew rich and positive
> From their ruinous landing, I'll attend disaster
> Like night birds over a wake, flying and live
> Above the shuttered house, and beautifully
> Wheel on the wing, find food in flight, and be
>
> Captured by light, drawn down and down and down
> By moonshine, streetlamps, windows, moving rays.
> By all that shines in all the caved-in town
> Where Mystic in the crazy moon outstays
> The death of Gods and makes a life of light
> That breaks, but calls a million birds to flight. (20–21)

Under the spell of this poem, it is easy to think that Ciardi never wrote a better. It stands in his work approximately as the Tintern Abbey poem does in Wordsworth's.

A look at the relatively obscure poems can prove instructive by contrast. Of necessity, there is a certain subjectivity in designating a work obscure. Perhaps it only needs the right reader. It is not always just profundity of thought, though one of the reviewers wished Ciardi would leave off philosophizing and remember that he was a poet; he found objectionable "the descent from the vital to abstraction of a general principle," which he regarded as the author's "greatest flaw as a poet."[13] The strain of fantasy streaked through Ciardi's work appears here in "The History of Something," which is faintly reminiscent of many poems by Kenneth Patchen. Nothing, or very little, seems to follow in this poem from anything else, which may be the principle exploited. If it is a correlative or analogue or allegory of any experience or idea, the present commentator has been unable to penetrate the secret. "Elegy in a Cube" uses the relations of forms in solid geometry—triangle, ellipses, circle and cube—which become "A holy family / In the dark of my own world's warping." The key may be in the lines, "These forms in a world of form / I found in a strictness of tears / At a withdrawal of time." The poem remains obscure, though not unappealing. "My General's Face," a weird kind of fantasy that may do no more than work out certain metaphors in fourteen lines, can also be charged with obscurity. Ciardi uses a construction such as ". . . I was the trunk / Of my standing in His eye'" in many poems, never with entire success. In "Shore Piece" we find "the sky's a lens under which / I am the amoeba of my own passing / Reflected in the blue eye of nowhere. . . ." Science or technology and theology become mixed in "High Tension Lines Across a Landscape." The power lines are regarded as "a way of ciphering God: / He is the highest socket and all his miracles / Are wired behind him. . . ." The first-person narrator, wet and naked, "Kissed that socket with my wet lip," whereupon "My teeth fell out, my fingers sprouted chives, / And what a bald head chewed on my sick heart." There is no recognizable human motive here; one must accept it as a natural occurrence in the surreal world of this poem. Since something called "God" figures in many of these poems, one would expect them to convey in some way a correlative for religious experiences, and that seems a likely approach to this one. If the poem is intended to leave no more than a sense of strangeness, then it is successful, but one wants more from a poem and from this poet who can give it when he chooses. However thoughtful these experiments may (or may not) be, they lack the warmth and vitality of his Italian poems. He discovered the possibilities of this subject in *From Time to Time*, and it has never failed him. The poems to his father are notable instances.

In prose and poem alike, Ciardi tells the story of the father who was killed in an accident when only son John was three, tells how his mother kept before him an image of the father he could not remember in fact, how in a sense he became his father, his mother's husband, and she in time became the son's daughter. The first reference to his father in *From Time to Time* comes in the meditative "Home Revisited: Midnight," but nothing is developed until the three poems, "Elegy I," "Elegy II," and "Elegy III, Cavalcante." In the first, the boy falls from the back of a truck into traffic, and, luckier than his father had been, survives.

There is a brief identification with his imagined father, that is soon to be lost in "the indifference of the healing to all but their wounds." Ciardi at this stage seems almost afraid to give way to emotion, perhaps for fear it would be like the self-pity of his childhood accident, though the image of his "Big Tony" invited emotion. His thoughts turned that way, however, when he was in a hotel "Thirty blocks and certain plausibilities / North of St. Michael's and my father's flower party." Here and in later poems he tells of the four hundred weeks of insurance checks "We ate him in." The third elegy is by far the best. He tells how his mother had raised him to avenge his father's death on Cavalcante, who "was a bad man, and, speeding, he killed my Father." He fantasized that vengeance at ages three and six and seven and twelve, already grown tall as urged. At twenty he was grown, and at thirty he had forgotten the whole thing, until the name came up again upon the man's death. Ciardi went to his wake and "stood by the death of the wreck that had been the blood / and error and evil of all my Mother's tears," at which time the dream of revenge came back too, in all of its stages.

The young man going through the mind of the man standing there might have been Childe Horvald on his way to just such a Dark Tower. Actually, one reviewer saw the poem "Childe Horvald" as autobiographical,[14] but it is better to take the poem literally. The character is merely a youth made obtusely idealistic by his elders. If in some way his experience parallels the author's, no less does it parallel that of any youth in brash innocence. It was no magic that changed Ciardi ("Or if you've real / Magic, change him! change him!"), or in any exclusive way, World War II; experience, of course, but most of all, one feels, the increasing experience of poetry itself.

These first efforts at recapturing the experience of the memory of the lost father are no less efforts at self-definition. Though Ciardi eventually visited Avellino, the place in Italy his parents had left in their teens, and though Italy evidently meant much to him personally and of course to his poetry, he did not pursue his family history much behind his parents. In his work, at least, he turned what he found back on himself, on what he knew, or remembered, had been told, or just responded to. That is the tap root to his poetic strength—personal experience. Yet one cannot escape the notion that in some way, personal rather than logical, Ciardi's work on Dante is one important result of his forays into

his own Italian past. If there was no literature, no capturable
glamor or romance or heroism other than survival under difficult
circumstances in the peasant past of his family, there was none
the less Dante, who was a sort of vindication. In his own mind,
one imagines, Ciardi became a spiritual stepchild of the great
Italian poet.

VI   As If *(1955)*

As If, subtitled *Poems New and Selected*, is one of Ciardi's most
appealing books. Of its seventy-three, twenty-eight are from the
three immediately preceding books; nothing is included from
Homeward to America. One might quibble over the selection,
but basically the book is a real accomplishment, showing good
poems from the past and adding excellent newer ones. The book
covers a wide range of thought and feeling, but Ciardi himself is
what holds everything together, not Ciardi as poet but Ciardi as
subject for the poet, his thought, his feelings, his impressions. He
has discovered once and for all how to use the personal yet not to
bore or disgust a reader who has his own problems with his own
subjectivity. Most of the poems are records of occasions in the life
of one of ours, a contemporary. For all of his claims that the poet
in speaking from the deepest depths of himself speaks for those
depths of each of us, it simply does not come about that way.
Instead, our response is more nearly sympathy and interest, even
fascination, rather than recognition and identification. Some of
the poems, after all, are not from the poet's depths but from the
top of his head. This does not make the poet any the less appealing. What he knows and presents to us, we know that much better; but what he experiences and presents to us, we are often not
able to participate in.

Nearly every reviewer grabbed Ciardi's remarks from the
dustjacket and offered them as though the book were explained.
"As if," the poet uttered vatically, "strikes me as the enduring
mode of poetry. IS is the mode of prose. Poetry is AS IF's reality.
When one has imagined ('lived as if') all his possibilities he may
begin to guess who he is and what world this is." Whether or not
Ciardi had "imagined all his possibilities," the poems in *As If*
show that he is aware that he is not a lesser Auden or Stevens. He
is a happy husband, a survivor of a war, an Italian-American
who has made a passionate pilgrimage to his parents' old home.

He is the widely read, brilliant intellectual, interested in the life about him, who appreciates it warmly if with irony, and seeks to bestow the poet's gift of immortality upon it by responding to it and letting it find the durable form of his words. He is interested in the world outside and the world inside and what each does to the other when they come together. If he is still interested in philosophy, that is, the general principles of things, it has a strong personal coloration. This could be a residue of the Stevens influence, but if so, it is what influences are properly for, how they should be used—to help a man broaden and deepen what is actually his own in the first place.

Also on the dustjacket was a remark Jazzman Sidney Bechet made when Ciardi wrote the musician's autobiography: "You tells it to the music and the music tells it to you. That's how you come to know what-all it is happened to you." What the poet made of the remark is some kind of dynamic synthesis between his intention and what the form and language of poetry will allow: each helps to create the other. Many of the poems have a casual, experience-of-the-moment effect about them, whereas in actuality the author was a laboring poet, capable of blotting a thousand lines. For all that, *As If* gives any proof that was needed that he was a poet who had for purposes of his art found himself.

As If begins with five untitled poems collectively called "To Judith," his wife, and more suitably considered in the discussion of *I Marry You* (1958), in which they are reprinted. These are followed by eight war poems, only one of which is new to this volume, "The Health of Captains." It has four rhymed quatrains. Key lines, one developed in each stanza, are "The health of captains is the sex of war," "The gloss of captains is the flags of war," "The deaths of captains are the tic of war," and ending rather than beginning the last stanza "The womb of woman is the kit of war." As a poem against war, it may succeed, in which case the grotesque or remote aspects and comparisons capture something of the grotesqueness of the experience of war. As here, there, and elsewhere in Ciardi's work, one feels that if he told *it* to this poem, the poem told it back too strong for him to manage successfully. The metaphors seem something to exploit by development rather than the necessary synthesis of responses to the subject.

A man grows older, and there is a new birthday poem in *As If*, "Poem for My Thirty-Ninth Birthday." The poem does not stretch to Ciardi's dimensions. Rather, it suggests, though in no profound way, the model of Dylan Thomas:

> I count my birthdays grave by grave, and stand
> watching the weather tremble to the storm
>
> that cooked all day while I strolled death by death
> by pools, by lawns, by sea, and all my loves.[15]

The acidulous Randall Jarrell in a review of *As If* put this and other similitudes together with the "as If" aesthetics to make a much harsher statement about Ciardi than is justified. Pointing like most early commentators to what he called Ciardi's "crude power," he observed further "the hesitations, reticences, and inabilities of the poetic nature—for to be able to say what it does say is to be unable to say everything else—are unknown to natures of such ready force, natures more akin to those of born executives, men ripe for running things." The statement seems to say more about the kind of poem Jarrell wrote than it does about its nominal subject. Jarrell borrows from psychologist Helene Deutsch for his intended *coup de grace*. As a poet Ciardi resembles, in her words as applied by Jarrell, "Persons of the 'as if' type, because in every new object-relation they live *as if* they were really living their own life and expressing their own feelings, opinions, and views."[16] Contrary to his usual practice, Jarrell singled out no poems for blame or praise. Apparent here is one of the troubles in considering writers before time has done its winnowing—literary politics may color even the critics' words. Luckily, there is not just one answer in poetry. A different critic could praise the "as if" phenomenon as an example of imagination, or why not the way Ciardi had put it, as a way for a poet to "begin to guess who he is and what world this is." Judson Jerome, for example, reviewed the book favorably and found Ciardi to be "a poet with more flexibility, more range, more depth, more solid achievement than any I know of who has emerged in the last ten or fifteen years." Indirectly the comment gave Ciardi credit for having achieved most of the aims set forth in the "Foreword to the Reader of (Some) General Culture" in *Live Another Day*, for having reached readers who would be valuable for poetry but had been turned away by poets' obscurities. Jerome singled out for praise the poet's individual tone of voice.[17]

The special qualities of that tone of voice are easiest to hear in Ciardi's Italian poems. In the section called "Tribal Poems" are two new poems on his father, "Elegy" and "To My Father." The first recapitulates in synoptic form his father's life, then gives, and then expounds in an idyllic style the dream held by the big man, just nicked here and there with irony:

> My father was born with a spade in his hand and traded it
> for a needle's eye to sit his days cross-legged on tables
> till he could sit no more, then sold insurance, reading
> the ten-cent-a-week lives like logarithms from
> The Tables of Metropolitan to their prepaid tombstones. (35)

From the pittances the collection man earned, he "bought / ten piney lots in Wilmington." Every Sunday he "took the train to his woods and walked under the trees / to leave his print on his own land, a patron of seasons." The narrator intrudes to tell us he has "done nothing as perfect as my father's Sundays / on his useless lots." Suddenly, the narrator tells us, "—Well, I have lied. Not so much lied as dreamed it." It was someone else, his sister, perhaps, who went on these expeditions to regain Paradise,

> But if it was her
> memory then, it became mine so long since
>
> I will owe nothing on it, having dreamed it from all
> the nights I was growing, the wet-pants man of the family.
> I have done nothing as perfect as I have dreamed him
> from old-wives tales and the running of my blood. (36)

The poem ends brilliantly, if ambiguously:

> But I will swear the world is not well made that rips
> such gardens from the week. Or I should have walked
> a saint's way to the cross and nail by nail
> hymned out my blood to glory, for one good reason. (36)

Curiously, one critic found fault with the entire last half of the poem, in effect a criticism of the structure. He commended the poet for revealing that the idyll was a waking dream and not actual experience, but "the effect of these lines is unfortunate. The first five stanzas, declared untrustworthy, become grotesque, part of an absurd comedy of paradox and introspection." He finds the last four lines, quoted above, to sound "a note of hysteria," to make "a desperate jump from the absurd to the sublime." Their sense is unrelated to what has gone before and therefore unsuccessful. Thus they merely add "to the grotesqueness of the poem."[18] Frankly, this is a poor reading of a rich poem. The unity of the poem is supplied by the narrator, and he is equally the subject with the deceased, hardly new in an elegy—vision and actuality and the significance of both. The real problem is the ambiguity of the last two and a half lines. Obviously they convey the passion that has not been possible in a world that would kill a man who dreamed big, such as his father. The narrator has already been undercut, as liar or fabulist and "wet-pants man of the family," and further twice designated as considerably less perfect than his vision of the lost father. Had the dream been allowed to live, the world would be different and the narrator would be different, too, perhaps capable of the sainthood he can only mention. Actually, the poem is rather simple but filled with a restrained passion and culminating in words both clear yet pregnant with emotion and appropriate meaning. It is one of Ciardi's splendid accomplishments. The mysteries of the father's death and its significances not only supplied him with material for several such poems but with enough ironies to last for a lifetime.

The poem "To My Father" is a meditation on death in relation to life. It is serious but not solemn. It has eighteen stanzas of three lines each, without rhymes. Several words are repeated in different contexts, "pebble," "stone," "sea," "gulls," "laughter," and others. This is to be one of Ciardi's substitutes for exact rhymes, to give him form within looseness. The lines tend to be prosey and loose ("When her child was born she bought him seven goats. . ."), but they can be intensified when wanted ("dip of the poppies' noon by a stone ruin"). The general movement of the poem is controlled by the pattern of nine end-stopped and ten run-on stanzas, as well as by varying the looser and the more concentrated lines. Basically, this is the technical situation in most of Ciardi's mature poems. Thematically, "To My Father" is a study in self-definition. The narrator watches the gulls as his father had watched them ("A big Italian man / . . . left me laughing / / with the taste of his stone in my mouth"). He could toss a pebble from the cliff or "pop it into my mouth like Demosthenes / to practice whatever is practiced by serious persuaders." Since he has "tasted the earth of that pebble," and by extension gained a knowledge of death, how can he come to

terms with it? On the basis of that knowledge, "I cannot believe
very much in sincerity." What to do? He could tell to the wind
the story of his father and the fathers back of that, or praise the
gulls "with the blood of every rape that stored my
fathers: / Greek, Turk, Moor, Hun, Goth, Visigoth—what
else?—" He adds the story of a wealthy Englishman near Salerno
who got a bastard on a local girl; with the father's money, she
bought him seven goats, from which by milk to cheese to song,
the bastard flourished and was happy. The narrator, "all proper,
right-handed and legal, / but as much my father's stranger" as
the goat boy was, ponders his purpose in life in relation to such
heritage. He addresses the father whom he has been told he
resembles. In a New England "whose history is also finished" but
with only "the Irishman's Boston" as heritage instead of a Rome,
he sees the heroical virtue as having come to nothing. The
implication of "I think we have been had in all good
humor / / you and I . . ." seems to be that the father should have
stayed in Italy close to his own, close to the legend of the laughing
goat boy. He hears laughter, as natural as water flowing out of
the earth, and then thinks of his father: "What are you doing
there sulking under the breakjaw / and final stone wedged in the
orator's mouth?" Again, how to reconcile the joy in life with the
knowledge of death? Despite his father's death, he knows that the
goats sustained the bastard to the point of "song / / he spilled to
the lifted gulls, as once they spilled / high from the wind on a sea-
berating Greek, / Old Logos with a bird turd on his bald spot."
The legend shows misfortune turned to a happy life, so the
possibility is there. There is no logic of life or of death that does
not include something of the other. The song of contentment goes
up to the gulls, and the gulls return it, from their process of
living, to any rationale of life or death, as a little gratuity , a
memento mori, an insult from life to death, from living to
thinking about living. As everywhere in Ciardi, we come upon a
duality when not a multiplicity, in which things are posed in
polar opposites yet held in the creative tension of a given poem.

   The issues confronted in this poem are the ironies of life in relation to death, and the methods for containing them in form lead
naturally to a consideration of "Thoughts on Looking into a
Thicket." It is an important credo in the author's development.
Jerome regarded it as representative of Ciardi's work at its best as

well as one of the finest new poems he had seen in years.[19] The poem is in seven unrhymed stanzas of eight lines each. A passage from English naturalist John Crompton's *Life of the Spider* is broken up into eight lines approximating the pentameter norm of the poem, with only the addition of the phrase "Writes Crompton." This is a device Ciardi uses several times in the course of his work. The fact that the prose set in the context of a poem can pass all but the most attentive reader as simply a stanza of the poem and within the range of its effects may be a sign of the poet's skill, but it is also an indication of the qualities of the poetic lines. Even if their casual and colloquial quality is controlled and functional, many lines nonetheless exist on the uncertain frontier between poetry and prose. Such an observation in no way detracts from "Thoughts on Looking into a Thicket," in which context the device has the air of a *tour de force*.

The thicket is not treated literally; instead the elaborate adaptations, purposes, and uses in nature, as posed by Crompton and recognizable immediately by any observant person as filled with larger meaning, are considered, in the way that Wordsworth treated certain natural objects when he thought he recognized in them a significance beyond their physical reality. Thus the thicket is life, simply, life in nature, but easily generalizable beyond that. The poem is a meditation, to begin with, on the nature of nature. Ciardi sets the scene with a condensed and representative recital of the adaptations for survival of insects and spiders: ". . . moths that look like leaves, like bark / like owls, like death's heads . . . eating flowers / and stones with eyes . . ." One of the incredible semblances is

> . . . a spider, *phrynarachne d.*,
> to whom a million or a billion years
> in the humorless long gut of all the wood
> have taught the art of mimicking a bird turd. (112)

The passage from Crompton is the next stanza and gives the details. Immediately accepting the rightness of the adaptations, the meditator moves to profounder thoughts. Where a person of easier disposition might resort to maxims like "God moves in mysterious ways," Ciardi puts it in a striking metaphor that has just the right allowance for error: "I read the rooty palm / of God

for the great scarred Life Line." Evidently the "proper people,"
whom Ciardi has ever contended against but has still taken into
consideration, condition the next lines:

> If you
> will be more proper than real, that is your
> death. I think life will do anything for a living.
>
> And that hungers are all one. (112)

Instances follow from another naturalist and the poet's own
observation, of a butterfly seemingly feasting but actually being
devoured, its flutters only serving to glut the devourer, and a
mantis feasting on a grub while in turn being consumed by a
copper beetle.

From these examples, we come to the conclusion in the form of
a credo. The words "I believe" and "I think" (in the sense of
believe) are repeated five times in fifteen lines. The immediate
conclusion of the ponderer is "So I believe the world // in its own
act and accomplishment. I think / what feeds is food." He moves to
an imaginary emblem for a "Church of the First Passion," the in-
terconnectedness of the impulse to survival without regard to
cost. He uses the old symbol of the Christian church, the fish,
which he images as a life line with each engorging the tail of the
one ahead of it. Thus, he would capture in symbol "our indi-
visible three natures in one: / the food, the feeder, and the condition of being / in the perpetual waver of the sea." In an
acknowledgement of the world which can be no other way, the
poet affirms, "I believe the world to praise it. I believe / the act
in its own occurrence." In the fact of the mutability that leads to
death, the poet affirms life. If it is grotesque, ugly, so is life. The
tone is solemn but resolved:

> . . . I believe
> if there is an inch or the underside of an inch
> for a life to grow on, a life will grow there;
>
> if there are kisses, flies will lay their eggs
> in the spent sleep of lovers; if there is time,
> it will be long enough. (113)

Death is remembered; a caressing hand stroking a beloved is a
memento mori. Mutability—there is no escape from it. Life, in

the context of this poem, feeds life, or devours life; it makes no difference:

> . . . my body eats me
> under the nose of God and Father and Mother.
> I speak from thickets and from nebulae:
> till their damnation feed them, all men starve. (113)

The survival theme in the war poems is almost trivial by comparison to the mature statement in this fully realized poem. One thinks that after such accomplishment so-called influences are best regarded as graceful acknowledgements of a response to another's work.

VII   I Marry You *(1958)—A Happy Marriage*

I Marry You is a relative failure in Ciardi's work. This is to regard it aesthetically and not otherwise, for it went into five printings in its first ten years. A critical reader can respond in a way that poses certain difficulties the poet encountered and may have solved in a less than entirely satisfactory way.

Something else that bothered the first commentators on the book was that Ciardi reviewed it himself in the *Saturday Review*, or rather, as he pointed out in one of those fine distinctions he had reason to know his readers of "(some) general culture" did not easily accept, "not exactly to review it, since a reviewer is more or less expected to say that the work is good or bad. . . ." He stated his intention for the book, and it is an acceptable description. For the rest, "whether these are good poems or bad must be left to the reader."[20] Contemporary reviewers gave enough negatives in the midst of their circumspect praise to cause one to say the book was a critical failure. Nearly everyone could commend the poet's intention and accept his analysis of *that*. Yet poems are realizations or they are nothing.

Ciardi's self-presented intention is something he had "long wanted to do," namely, to put together "a little sheaf of love poems, some new, some gathered from earlier books, made into a poetry-diary of a happy marriage. . . ." With the touch of irony that is never beyond his reach, he notes that there is "not an Important Poem in the batch, but only poems for my wife's and my children's and my remembrance as the world changes out from under us." Of necessity, these poems are private, but one of the author's deepest convictions about his personalism is offered as qualification. To be private and nothing else would offer no justification for the volume. The poet's aim, as separated from the husband's, was "to find the private center of this marriage so truly that the poems will touch some part of everyone's truest privacy. I think all poetry must try to find that center."[21] Few if any of the poems achieve this ideal and, certainly, the book does not.

Much of the general problem with *I Marry You* is how to write love poetry in an age that is uncertain what love should be in fact and does not accept it as theme for serious art. In medieval Provence and Italy, then later in Renaissance France and England, major poets could write poems on love themes without the hindrance of the modern self-conscious questioning of the propriety of the act, without the modern poet's fear of personal emotion, without the near terror that the after-all unavoidable emotion might be excessive and therefore sentimental. There was no living tradition to sustain the poet of the 1950s with this theme, despite notable poems by William Butler Yeats and a few others, such as Conrad Aiken, William Carlos Williams, and Kenneth Patchen. Yet where was the modern poet whose work was unimaginable or greatly diminished without the theme of love, as Donne's would have been? The nineteenth century offered no help; Rossetti, Patmore, and Mrs. Browning were unconvincing in their excesses. The seventeenth century was the last place a modern poet could seek guidance in the handling of such a theme, Donne in particular, since Ciardi's subject was married love and the tensions between body and soul (however defined), as well as the harmonies. The assumption here is that Donne offered Ciardi a similar sense of the extremes and disparities in his experience of the subject that must be reconciled in the poems, if modern means can be found. The answer was easier in the religious context of the seventeenth century because the intellectual framework included such extremes already. Ciardi's efforts might be the more heroic, the more certain to fail because of the secular assumptions with which he had to work.

Ciardi's big problem in the poems is to present certain of the *biedermeier* virtues yet avoid the too personal, the sentimental, the entirely private emotion. In the intensity of his passions, the poet may here do something that is a source of failure in other poems as well. He conjures with words beyond the reader's ability to follow. The words seem bigger than the subject. As Arthur Symons said of Byron, he writes like a man whose tongue is too big for his mouth. Ciardi does what Wordsworth said the poet must do; he must add the emotion to the poem, presumably by his responses to it. The problem is that the reader can doubt (though possibly in error) that they are really true for the poet. In love poems especially this amounts to a breach of "the sympathetic contract" (Ciardi's term in *How Does a Poem Mean?*) between reader and poet. "As If" too easily becomes, "Yes, I know, but. . . ." Actually, Ciardi's approach works well enough in several poems, for example, in "Men Marry What They Need. I Marry You." Even if one doubts the generalization, it is sufficiently redeemed by the next phrase, "I Marry You." The subjectivity is allowable, even in its semblance of objectivity, though a single false step would throw this *Heldenleben* into the mock-heroic mode and ruin the entire poem. It is harder in these poems than in any by the author to separate what is said from formal concerns, that is, hard not to commend what Ciardi says, if one approves, no matter how he says it. Convinced and convincing hyperbole is the mode of love poetry; poems celebrating marriage, few as they are, are generally quieter. The poem under consideration, reprinted from *From Time to Time* and *As If*, is given as a kind of prologue to the rest of the volume, separated from it by the table of contents. Or better, it is the first entry in the diary. Either way, it serves as virtually an epigraph for the whole.

How literally one is to take the line ". . . every marriage makes this marriage new" may be questioned, but the Donne similitude is recognizable. The finest lines (and also most to be admired for their content) come as a counterpoise to images of mutabilty:

> I marry you from time and a great door
> is shut and stays shut against wind, sea, stone,
> sunburst, and heavenfall.[22]

James Wright made a proper objection to the words "sunburst" and "heavenfall": "What a relief it would be if Mr. Ciardi would only let the two magnificent lines alone! But no. Wind, sea, stone are not enough for him; he had to add 'sunburst and heavenfall' to his list. I think these two Hopkinsisms (an ugly word for an ugly effect) ruin Mr. Ciardi's lines just as those lines have begun to find their characteristic beauty—their simplicity, humanity, strength." And this is one of the problems with the entire book. This quality of "fine excess" is beyond what the reader in this context, even with the most willing faith, is able to participate in. If two words can ruin a poem, then the poem is ruined despite the redemption of other whole lines like those which follow, after again confronting the emblems of mutability ("Why should I bother / the flies about me? Let them buzz and do."), and show, as Wright put it, "the clarity of the music and the depth of the emotion are splendidly fused"[23]:

> Men marry their queen, their daughter, or their mother
>
> by names they prove, but that thin buzz whines through:
> when reason falls to reasons, cause is true.
> Men marry what they need. I marry you. (v)

Two nature poems show other aspects of the book. James G. Southworth said "Snowy Heron" was Ciardi's "most perfect poem," one in which he "most nearly effects a perfect fusion of thought and form."[24] It is one of its author's many affirmations of life: "What lifts the heron leaning on the air / I praise without a name." In the context of the marriage volume, to praise outer life is not to leave the inner.

The same reverent attitude toward life appears in "Two Egrets" where the epigraph " 'Look!' you said. 'Look!' " makes the connection between perception and the transformed nature of the experience because it exists in the context of the shared experience of marriage. Again, as in "Snowy Heron," living beauty in the form of graceful birds, seen on Easter morning, is the basis of the poem. The birds are compared to "two white hands / washing one another / in the prime of light." The reverent ending calls the "white stroke" of the birds, followed by the eye "as high as the eye dizzies," "a prayer / and the idea of prayer" (17). Presumably the birds correspond to the prayer, but what is the "idea of prayer"? Is it not the eye following them beyond its capacities to see any longer in the fathomless deeps of the sky?

If this poem with this ending came into an accepted religious context, it would be no more than a commonplace observation. Taken by itself, even with the epigraph, it can be mere psychology. The narrator and the other observer share an experience that moves them in their minds to reverent thoughts; the important thing would be the accuracy to perception and to the psychological response. But in the context of a marriage book in which everywhere abounds the exaltation of the simplest acts of the lovers, one looks for the elevation in every poem. The sensibility made luminous (not necessarily spiritual) by marriage responds in a new way to everything. D. H. Lawrence did a similar thing in his cycle of marriage poems, "Look! We Have Come Through!" Has Ciardi achieved this for the reader? His difficulty is that if the well-disposed reader does not make certain connections for him, then on aesthetic grounds the poems could often be accounted failures, despite the brilliant effects. Thus, a title or epigraph often forces an interpretation of a single poem that might otherwise be missed. The entire context of *I Marry You* does supply much of what is needed.

War is a backdrop for certain of the poems as in "Epithalamion After a War" and "Ten Years Ago When I Played at Being Brave." The marriage took place in the former, "by a ritual of legality" (rather than of sacrament). Part of the structure of the poem is to play the unreality of legality off against the reality of legalized marriage as experienced.

The other poem haunted by war puts the daily risk of flaming death in the war and its self-pitying thought of a last wish before dying against his own attainment in life of that fulfilled dream in the form of the ultimate woman, his wife. The poem is a graceful tribute that edges the sentimental adroitly. If it is not an "Important Poem," the author has already warned us.

A more successful poem is "To Judith Asleep." Unlike the last poem, this one begins better than it ends. Southworth singled it out as one of the four best in the volume; John Thompson found it most at fault. The husband-lover stares at the naked beauty of his sleeping wife in the moonlight. She is "all let down / in ferny streams of sleep and petaled thighs / rippling into my flesh's buzzing garden." Thompson found Ciardi's intensity to be "heavy as a ton of bricks," and in a witty, imaginary dialogue between an admirer and a nonadmirer found this poem especially objectionable. Speaking of the above lines, the nonadmirer denies that he is squeamish in regard to "real physical stuff," but objects: " . . . Well, if only it weren't a garden. And then, if it weren't buzzing, like a pail full of flies. And, well, if only, if only it

weren't *his*. Maybe if he were talking about somebody else . . ."
He objected, further, to other lines that make the case just as
strong *for* Ciardi, as the admirer seeks to do:

> Far and familiar your body's myth-map lights,
> traveled by moon and dapple. Sagas were curved
> like scimitars to your hips. The raiders' ships
> all sailed to your one port (6).

The nonadmirer, who is accused of being too fussy by the admirer, evidently regards the "one port" to be the same as Donne
in "To His Mistress Going To Bed," when he speaks of "O My
America! my new-found-land" or the "hairy Diadem." Perhaps
the nonadmirer is right, although the metaphor of "port" is not
confined to that single meaning. The bemused husband sees
himself as "Bravo and monk (the heads and tails of love) / . . . a
spinning coin of wish and dread," in fear that death should take
her and leave him bereft of the "mystery sudden as you are / a
light on light in light beyond the light." The dramatic situation
perfectly justifies words that cannot be objectively justified.
"Child, child," he addresses her in his thoughts, and wishes for
her to be undisturbed in her sleep, but living. The ending continues the mood of tenderness that is at least as important as the
tough sexuality: "My dear of all / saga and century, sleep in
familiar-far. / Time still must tick *this is, I am, we are.*" Thompson, merging with his nonadmirer, concluded, "There is good
baroque poetry in the world. John Ciardi has not written it."[25]
It would be fairer to say, at least of the ending of 'To Judith
Asleep," that the poet has found a bastion which Death may top-
ple in the future but is invulnerable moment by living moment.
The poem partakes of Ciardi's typical secular affirmation of the
here and now, which nonetheless shirks neither past nor future.
The poem may not be beyond reproach, but it is rich enough to
withstand critical assaults.

The Donne influence is seen at its most acceptable in "Most
Like an Arch This Marriage," which Southworth identifies
among the four best. The poem employs four rhymed quatrains.
The poem exploits aspects of the arch metaphor—an entrance,
"Mass made idea, and idea held in place," "A lock in time," inside
of which "half-heaven unfolds." Always there is mutability:
"World as it is, / what's strong and separate falters." Separate,

each half of the arch is "roofless around nothing," but joining in the symbol of a kiss, ". . . we make / the all-bearing point, for one another's sake, / in faultless failing, raised by our own weight." The Donne quality appears especially in the paradox of falling whereby raising the arch to its strength.

Three children come of the marriage. They are part of the background of "Letter from an Empty House," a straightforward poem of a kind Ciardi can write at every stage of his career. The poem is about no more than the loneliness of the husband and father in the now-strange house when the wife and children are gone for two weeks. Nothing is familiar any longer. The emptiness of the house and the emptiness of the man correspond. With no tricks, no rhetoric, not even any thoughts of death, the author writes a moving if simple poem. Where often he conjures with words, here all he has to do is represent. The quiet house is adequate objective correlative for the emptiness within. It is not sentimental despite the many opportunities to become so. Even the reader of no general culture could participate in this quiet poem.

"A Suite for Love" in seven sections is not the least considerable poem in the book, but it adds nothing by theme or other quality that has not been set forth already. The one poem in the collection that might be regretted is "Letter from a Death Bed." The poem is a kind of dramatic monologue (though its title says "Letter"), imagining the last farewell between dying narrator and the beloved. The poem is Browningesque, extremely colloquial in manner. Life and love have been praised from various perspectives, including Death as imagined. But this poem is literal. One must deliberately withdraw from it and think of the idea of it in context in order to accept it as an integral part of the sheaf of love poems called *I Marry You.*

CHAPTER 3

Years of Solid Achievement

I 39 Poems (1959)

3 9 *Poems* was called a failure by James G. Southworth, in a concise but comprehensive essay on Ciardi's poetry in 1961: "His latest volume, *39 Poems*, largely satirical, often deeply perceptive, and inherent with the stuff of poetry, contains no poem that will withstand a sharp critical analysis, no poem in which the various elements of a poem are fused into really significant form. If his is a conscious choice of the immediate plaudits of the uncritical I have no quarrel with him"; but if Ciardi was to survive as a poet, Southworth felt, he should "subject himself to a severe questioning of his motives, purposes, and goals."[1] If earlier Ciardi was luckier than most aspiring poets in being noticed by established and influential poets and critics, now his success seems to be rather at the popular level, for *39 Poems* went into a third printing within its first five years.

Interviewed in 1974, Ciardi mentioned one of his books then in press which he had submitted to "A very good friend, whose criticisms I generally value, and he decided it was a disaster. He didn't like it. I walked the floor with that damned manuscript for three weeks, just reading it to myself, trying to decide whether I should or should not take his advice, and finally I decided that it was not my poems he disliked—it was my lousy character. Every one of the poems expressed my character."[2] This is as true of *39 Poems* as of any Ciardi volume. As sign at least of the author's esteem, he once again wrote a notice in the *Saturday Review* of the appearance of one of his books (not review, he insisted, also again); he had already published one of the poems, "Bridal Photo, 1906," with a detailed individual commentary.

One can see why, despite Ciardi's "careful disclaimer" that he was not reviewing *I Marry You* because "a review implies some judgment of merit or lack of merit," that within a month he had received more than a hundred letters about his "arrogance in assuming that no one else was equipped to review the output of my swollen ego."[3] Ciardi was right, of course, by his standard of review (which at the time of the *Unicorn* controversy in 1957 he stated explicitly), but for most readers, of whatever degree of culture, any notice of a book in print, regardless of what is said, passes for a review. That first self-promotion had been a modest half-column under the section heading "Poetry," while the notice of *39 Poems* dominates a page with the title in large letters, "Poetic Violence in Three Parts." Especially as Ciardi did "happily confess" to his readers that it was "fun to stir up the beast" in them, one suspects at least one motive was to supply the columnist with material for part of his dialogue with his audience in the form of protests. This time he was even more scrupulous in confining his comments to his intentions and just as scrupulous in leaving the judgment elsewhere: "That I have tried to write well, I will declare to any man. Whether or not I have done so rests within any reader's judgment." He explained, too, that as poetry editor he would have had to choose the reviewer and pass judgment on the result before it appeared in the magazine. Since it was unavoidably an inside job, "Let it, therefore, be declaredly an inside job."

The author's description of his book offered a provisional artistic credo that is consistent with his other statements to this effect, early and late, and thus bespeaks a consistency of intention and suggests a rough unity for the entire body of work. As mentioned earlier in this study, it is easy to accuse Ciardi of excesses of several kinds, including self-indulgence and loss of control over his material. But as nearly every poet has done, he pointed out that, "In a sense, no one chooses the poems he will write. The poems choose him as they come, and he struggles to make them firm." He admitted to a compulsion to violence, but denied knowledge of the reasons. And he quoted approvingly Dudley Fitt's identification of "violence joined to control" as central in his writing. The poet acknowledged the one and claimed to have labored for the other.

In general, Ciardi speaks up for form as strongly as he speaks up for subject finding its own form, but there is no real conflict. Subject for him is not something outside the poet; rather it is the interaction between what is outside and the poet's response. If poems choose him, it is because his responses are already the raw material for the poem.Plato's *Ion* with a relatively mindless performer serving as vehicle for what he may not even understand is far from Ciardi's conception.

Another statement appears here that would form part of Ciardi's comprehensive credo. The first group of poems in *39 Poems* is called "In Ego with Us All." What he intended to express was his recurrent idea that "what is personal to any man becomes, when it is pursued deeply enough, personal to every other." Who could ask more modest qualification than "I may not have carried it deeply enough, but that is a question of performance, and I am here describing intent"? Fair enough. Whether for this reason or others, readers (to judge from critical commentaries) seem more to respond to Ciardi's poems with interested sympathy than with identification. Most of the time, one likes the tough Italian kid who can handle himself in any situation, but someone with a different background and sensibility is not compelled by the work to participate beyond sympathy.

If this is true, it does not make Ciardi any the less the poet, but it does qualify his achievement in relation to his stated aim, which is really more a matter of faith than of intent in the logical sense, a faith that allows him to exploit the personal with the confidence that it is more than personal.

The satirical poems to which Southworth refers make up the second section of the book, "In the Year of the Longest Cadillac." Their author denominates them "social poems," admittedly borrowing the term from an earlier time which used it for "comments on the state of the world," something never far from Ciardi's consideration. The difference between these and other Ciardi poems is that few of these are personal; their form is often objective or dramatic (as opposed to the personal and lyrical), and the several characters who bear the burden of the themes are not simply personae for the author.

The third section of the book is called "Certainties." Most of the poems are about art and artists. Some of the poems are written to the author's personal friends, but then so are some of the poems in section one. Thus his statement of intentions makes distinctions that are truly more of intent than of fact. But there is no cavil with his belief that art "is a certainty men can live by. Could we find a world as good and as orderly and as meaningful as art, we should all have the certainty of sound values to live by.

It is the world that confuses; art assures. It must do so over and over again, but always it brings that certainty into view again." The author is again in the realm of faith and hope as far as his own poems are concerned. His repeated position as to whether he has achieved any of these values is that it must be left to readers to decide for themselves.

To turn to the poems, apart from the author's general intentions for them collectively, we find in the first section of one of Ciardi's family poems, "Bridal Photo, 1906," provoked by a picture of his parents on their wedding day.[4] Before its appearance in this book, he had published it with a commentary in the IBM's house organ, *Think*.[5] Of his several commentaries on his own work, this is the best. I have several times accused Ciardi of conjuring with words so that the result is an illusion, despite his commitment to the world as it exists, of creating a poem out of words alone, the seeming emotions not really behind them. Any such tendency is gloriously transcended in "Bridal Photo, 1906," as in most of the poems about his parents and his Italian background, for here feeling and form come together in a near-flawless consummation. With the essay, though not in the book, he reprints the photo. The poem, in what it says, may or may not achieve the ultimate human depths, but to the extent that an approach is made in this poem, the profundity is achieved unself-consciously. The narrator is so rapt in his response to the picture he forgets all else—as indeed he should. There is something archetypal about looking in a glass or a picture that in some way speaks of the self; it might be the image floating on a pool of water, a picture of oneself in an appearance and at an age one does not remember, or a picture of one's forbears one scans for resemblance, for the human mystery. The Narcissus theme from antiquity comes immediately to mind, as do the Enchanted Glass of the Elizabethans, Lewis Carroll, and more modern instances like Rilke, Robert Graves, and others. Ciardi's poem is in nine unrhymed stanzas of five lines each. His essay is entirely thematic and personal—and worth following.

He begins with a statement about a poet's working aesthetics that is considerably more sophisticated than the "Foreword to a Reader of (Some) General Culture" of ten years earlier. Obviously, he has thought about the nature and practice of poetry from his own experience but also from his work on the textbook *How Does a Poem Mean?*, soon to appear. He insists, as all poets do, there is no "explanation" that will in any way substitute for a poem; it is "itself." A poem is *"something happening"* rather than merely *"something said about something."* In so far as words can do it, a poem must capture an experience, embody it rather than tell that it happened; and the reader must experience it too, as nearly as possible. There is no room for illusionism here, though all the room for artistry there ever was. Looking at the photo, Ciardi says, he "sensed possibilities" in this theme. He had seen the picture all of his life, but in the new moment of perception realized that this couple, "so much a part of my being," exemplified "the unblinkable fact that they are truly strangers to me." He saw not just a problem of his own identity but "a question of the identity of all life, link by link in the chain of Adam, back to all beginning and Everyman." Distance was necessary to preserve the duality of closeness yet strangeness. The first two stanzas describe objectively the solemn couple at a moment in their nuptials, or in the author's words "an almost coldly sociological observation." The description picked up the appurtenances—"ceremonial rose," "horseshoe wreath of pearls," "gold watch," "gold locket"—as though the people were "some sort of tribal notables in full ceremonial regalia." This suggestion of the tribal—a recurrent metaphor of Ciardi's when he talks about family in the context of time—does not hold the same emotions for a reader as for the author. The third stanza questions the tableau: "What moment is this frozen from their lives / as if a movie stuck in its lit tracks?"

The metaphor of the movie from which one frame survived "led immediately to the next movement of the poem which is an effort to reimagine that total movie from which this one moment survives." Stanzas 3–5 take up the rest of the bridal day. Three important points in that day were the church, the bridal, and the photographer's studio; in the poem they are "the priest's gilt cave," "their new bed," and "the rigged cave / of the unknown hooded man." With the photograph before him, the author has an emblem like that of Keats and his Grecian urn, an emblem that opens back into the past as far as people go, and the other way for the future. The poet knows the next steps into the future, however:

> I follow this long look into its dark
> where, leathered as an Indian chief, the woman

> sags through this lace to keen for the bashed corpse
> that drops from the man's steadiness in his hour.

Or in more prosaic details which the essay gives, "the man died, bashed and bloody, in an auto wreck 13 years later." The woman was near eighty at the time of the writing, "still of the tribe but now of its ruin and antiquity rather than of its flower time . . . an ancient shriveled woman now almost 40 years his widow." The hooded man's photograph held in his hand, his mind "darkened by knowledge," the narrator offers a prayer "to that held hour from its last love" (John was the last child);

> *Bless the unfinished bridal to its bed.*
> *This day becomes this day. What others follow*
> *have touched their flower. By all flowers and all fall*
> *I am the son of this man and this woman.*

The distance is bridged. The narrator is the continuator in the great tradition of love, at one with all lovers and their risks, out of which all human possibilities arise.

The essayist singles out "This day becomes this day" as possibly difficult for the reader. Since every element has a double meaning, the sentence provides an excellent example of the meaningful ambiguity the poet espoused a decade earlier. He intended, with the nice qualification "I think," these meanings:

> This day (of the bridal) becomes (passes into) this day (of my looking back from years later).
> This day (of the bridal) becomes (befits, honors, is appropriate to) this day (itself).
> This day (of my looking back) both passes into and befits (as an act of identification and love) this day (of the bridal). (21)

Three aspects of the poem are picked up, respectively, by the three meanings: "the dark thought," "the flowering thought," and the "justifying thought: the love that justifies love in the chain of man and woman." Out of the last, "intending a final affirmation that stays valid for me," he was able to come up with the last line of the poem. From the experience of the poem, the essayist tells us, he emerged "knowing more and more truly about myself, and about all of us."

This poem is one of the better examples of Ciardi's use of personal themes that aspire to take in all of humanity, that which is to be found in the deepest recesses of the experience of any person. Regardless of whether he has reconstructed accurately his creative process, he has very nearly succeeded in the larger aim. A reader would probably not respond quite as profoundly as the author—he might prefer his own parents or grandparents—but the poem is successful enough to show the general validity of its author's idea and that at his best he is very nearly capable of achieving it. In the poem "In Ego with Us All," the poet tries, explicitly, for these same things but with much less success, though the poem is by no means inconsiderable.

The poem "Abundance" shows the poet using a method that is typical of his mature technique. One aspect is the seeming looseness of many lines, a flatness indistinguishable from prose: "Once I had 1000 roses. / Literally 1000 roses. I was working for a florist / back in the shambling 'Thirties . . . " To put a positive interpretation on the choice, such lines are often used to provide exposition necessary to set up later intensities; also, they are sometimes part of the control of pace in a poem. A reader could still object that, though the lines might pass as conversation, a poem requires better. At the same time, Ciardi rarely relaxes his control for long (if that explains what happens here). Another quality of "Abundance" is to turn conventions upside down, in this case the symbolism of red and white roses. The narrator intended that the five hundred red roses and five hundred white, which he bought "for Connie's wedding to steadiness" and strewed all down the church aisle, should be interpreted to symbolize "White for the bed we had shared. / Red for the bed she went to / from the abundance in her / to the fear in what she wanted."

He adds that "The gift was not in the roses / but in the abundance of the roses." Thus the word "abundance" is used twice within four lines in the second stanza of ten lines. It appears twice in the next three lines in positive and negative aspects (as a repetition it counts even when qualified by "no"). The gift of the abundance of roses was to the bride "whose abundance had never wholly / been mine, and could never be his. / He had no gift of abundance in him, / but only the penuries of sobriety." In the narrator's view, the groom would be walking "over the most flowering he would ever / touch, the the most flowering I / had ever touched. A feast of endings." "Flowering" is already associated with the roses and the gesture, both being extravagant, "abundant," and all culminate in "A Feast of endings," with which section one of the poem concludes.

In section 2 the narrator, in the present, this morning passed a cart heaped with white carnations and is reminded of the snows of childhood heaped up in a fullness that provokes the imagination. He images himself, bursting with energy, as a young wolf in its prime, cavorting in the snow. Moving this image into the reflective present, he concludes: "There is no feast but energy. All men / know—have known and will remember / again and again—what food that is / for the running young wolf of the rare days . . ." when any attainment wanted—snapping snowflakes from the air—is accessible to the wolf's energy. He has wandered away in this second section to experiences that, in chronology, are prior to the experience with Connie; yet he has come to lines that would seem to be a kind of analogue for that response too: the snapped snowflakes that " . . . are instantly nothing— / a commotion in the air and in the blood. /—And how they are endlessly all." The connection between the young wolf and the narrator when young, if not self-evidently an abundance, a feast, is made specifically in "There is no feast but energy," in that both theme and the word itself are repeated.

Another association with snow and flowers begins section 3; it is his father's grave, "banked with snow and lilies." The wind tore them apart and blew the petals away like snowflakes, whereby they became "A last / abundance correcting our poverties." The word "remember" is used five times in the next five lines; feasts are mentioned twice, the wolf once. The father is seen as "a man of abundance"; the flowers blowing in the air try "to make the winter clean again in air," to no avail. The young wolf has matured from his days of "abundance" to "the ravening of recollection." So the flowers blowing from the grave are like the flowers strewn at the wedding, and both are like the memories of abundances and losses.

Section 4 returns to the pushcart heaped with flowers in the present, "heaped beyond possibility. . . ." The enchanted snowscapes of childhood memory are invoked again, in different terms but"—At a corner of the ordinary." Where is the girl now? Gone like the remembered snows, the young wolf, the dead father. All have become "A feast of glimpses. Not fact itself, / but an idea of the possible in the fact." This section, which concludes the poem, brings all of the themes together; they culminate in proclaiming the advent of a new love, quite possibly on the narrator's own wedding day. He is again the young wolf, in his intensity, and "profusions" come "in their instant next to the ordinary." "Feast" is mentioned twice in the stanza, "profusion" and "plenty" once each.

Perfection, the narrator surmises, must be brief; this brevity is played off against "The long thing," which is " . . . to remember / imperfectly, dirtying with gratitude / the grave of abundance." The new woman brings all of the themes together and both redeems and fulfills what was only partial in the past. Words are repeated from section 2 with slight variation and new meaning:

> O flower-banked,
> air-dazzling, and abundant woman,
> though the young wolf is dead, all men
> know—have known and must remember—
> You. (7)

More words and ideas are repeated in this poem than can be shown without quoting the five pages in full, but enough has been pointed out to show that, in the midst of a seeming looseness, there are richness and concentration in veritable "abundance."

Part II of *39 Poems*, "In the Year of the Longest Cadillac," is the collection of "political" poems. Despite his campaigning for Henry Wallace in 1948, Ciardi is not basically a political man. This is not to say that opinions on many political or larger social issues are absent from his work. He is acutely attuned to present-day happenings, whether they touch him personally or not, and to their significance at the level of generality. Mockery, irony, contempt, sarcasm, invective, reductio ad absurdum, one would expect to find in the work of any poet with such concerns. Several reviewers singled these poems out for praise; or was it the attitudes behind them? The present writer does not share these views of Ciardi's "political" verse. While most of it is more accomplished than the attack on literary coteries in *From Time to Time*, it is still not his best vein. Political matters seem to touch his mind only and not to engage the entire person, even when he finds his general conclusions about mankind and the state of the human condition confirmed. The public poems rarely engage the whole, passionate person Ciardi is and which is of the essence of his finest poems. The theme of war is a mild exception, but war as an idea which the poet abominates is different from the war that daily risked the life of a brash young machine-gunner named John Ciardi—and the poems reflect the difference, quality being preponderantly with the latter.

Several of these poems show antiwar aspects. One of the better is "Of Heroes Home from Troy and More Coming." The survivors were "small ones," who grew taller as their stories were retold. They were not heroes, but seen through death they become so. They, the earliest of such survivors we have literary record of —boys in the race of men in general—must be allowed as heroes because they set the standard of "what a man must be seen by." Imagining them home, the race creates the glory for them. The narrator intrudes in the first person with a two-line commentary at the end: "Ah, how we wish to be beyond weather / and inconsolables, crazy for glory and God!" The lines are subject to two readings. Does "crazy for glory and God" go with the "inconsolables," or does it go with "how we wish to be"? If the former, then why the comma? Just for a pause? If we were beyond them, then we could see wars and the heroic myths truly. In which case, who is included in "we"? Suppose, on the other hand, that the "we" is all of us, as members of the human race. We wish to be beyond the flucuations of weather and apart from those who cannot accept the idea of the glory of the survivors because of their own griefs; we wish to accept the myth of the glory and of the divine purpose of wars, even though we create them ourselves. Because the poem picks up an essential cleavage in the human breast and sets it forth adequately, this poem is superior to the satirical ones.

"The Baboon and the State," unpleasant though it is, may be the best of the gibing poems. A dog-snouted baboon "puzzles out the look of a man." At the smell of a stranger, the beasts rally around a conception of their superiority: "Born of the chosen, first, and tallest tree! / Sons of the Sacred Banyan follow me! / Baboons are born to kill because they can." The poem adds dimension by a stanza each to Clemenceau and Wilson at the World War I peace conference; to Guido da Montefeltro, who counseled Pope Boniface VIII on the means to destroy the Colonna family in 1297; and to "seven-minded" Odysseus, who

"Piled up his kills to honor prophecy— / An indispensable, most Ithacan / Justification for a blood at war." He "heard God-talk on the air . . . " The narrator asks the questions which may be the logical point of the poem: "Is man wrong for the State, or it for man? / High reasons and low causes make a war." Further, "It is the Baboon kills, because he can . . ." meaning also that anything that kills is a baboon; but Presidents, like the baboons of stanza one, also "hear voices from the air," with the result that packs of apes not less than parishes of men cry out with a sense of divine certitude. However, "The voices come to rest where they began." Clemenceau and Guido repeat their actions of earlier stanzas, and "An indispensable most Ithacan / Baboon snout puzzles out the look of a man. / The killers kill. They kill because they can." The poem is about the base causes of things, nothing less really than the corruption by power. It puts together the bestial in which power is the norm with the human in which it is frequent. The human creature as represented by one legendary and two historical notables is different only in the lies of his rationalizations.

Two narrative poems that appear in this section deserve mention: "Captain Nicholas Strong" and "Ulysses." Though the poet handles the narrative elements skillfully, it is the theme of human responses to war that puts these two poems in their context in 39 *Poems.*

"Captain Nicholas Strong" is the story of an American civilian doing military duty in World War II. The greatest thing that happened to him in the war was the liberation by his unit of a German concentration camp that was surrendered by the three last guards. When the captain saw the hideous condition of the inmates, "He took two drinks / and shot the guards himself." The description of the freed inmates eating flour by the handful from barrels, gagging, choking, cramming it again into starved maws is vivid. The protagonist liberated other groups of the damned, but none so impressed him as the first. Curiously, he hated the survivors more than the guards:

> their stink, their burls of bone, their slimey beards:
> they clung to life so hard they dirtied it.
> He would have shot them sooner than the guards
> had he been God. The Captain *had* to kill:
> only a violence could wash him. (64)

His only requirement in each killing was "that his face must never move." Returning to civilian life as the proprietor "—of all things—Nick Strong's Haberdashery," he never quite got over that first encounter with realities he could not compass. The omniscient narrator connects him to the reader, but with caution: "What part / of anything the Captain was in Hell / is all of us in time, I do not know." Do we too participate in this fate? The captain is obviously a kind of war lover, somewhat like the central character in John Hersey's novel *The War Lover*, seemingly an American Liberal discovery of the time. In so far as Ciardi had ever been a liberal of the simple beliefs that war and other problems stem from external causes that can be remedied by the right governmental social programs and the like, he had paid for it by the war experiences in which he, innocent of real malice, had participated in the destruction of hundreds of thousands even more innocent. Whether from that or whatever, he had come, as "Captain Nicholas Strong" shows, to a profounder view of evil in which, in our degree, all of us are implicated. The captain bears the perplexity and confusion of Americans with their cowboy-and-Indians morality, their clean-cut view of life, their lack of self-knowledge. The war is a means of fulfilling a part of the Captain's nature, an unsatisfactory and perhaps a partial one. Wrenched by reality beyond the limits of that morality, the soldier, who is really someone like you, good old Nick down at the haberdashery, has no resources within himself that can respond otherwise. He is more like the guards than like the inmates. It might be possible to say the poem is about the corruption of an innocent by war, but it has been read here as a commentary on not just innocence but on the well-springs of human nature (the "foul rag and bone shop of the heart," Yeats called it), with just a margin of hope in that we and the captain may not be identical. The poem has the moral effect (and presumably the moral intention) of causing the reader to peer into his own depths if only to see whether he finds Captain Nicholas Strong, the once and present haberdasher lurking there, waiting only the right opportunity to spring into action.

"Ulysses," despite the narrative mode, has thematic links with both "Captain Nicholas Strong" and "The Baboon and the State." All three ponder the certitude that leads men to war—and to unintended consequences, one of which is a self-knowledge from which may be generalized the human situation. An important

difference from the other two poems is that the character Ulysses
tells his own story. Whatever smaller purpose the author might
intend is thus cast into the whirlpool along with other elements of
a character, if he is fairly rendered. It might be said that Ciardi
here puts on the mask of Ulysses, but a character is more than a
mask. Also, Ciardi is enough of a modern poet (or a particular
kind of modern poet) to let things and persons speak for themselves, no doubt in hope they will say what he wants said but yet
committed to letting them have their say no matter how it goes.
Ciardi seems to use the story of the death of Ulysses that Dante in-
vented in the *Inferno* in Canto xxvi. Thus at his end, "at the last
mountain" (the Mountain of Purgatory, in Dante's poem),
Ulysses is vouchsafed something from nature for his end that at
the same time is a correlative for his life. "Was this my life?" he
asks himself. Instead of the sea he remembers, this is "something
from an augur's madness: / sheep guts, bird guts, ox guts, smok-
ing / in a hot eye." He remembers that he had followed the
prescribed rituals. An oaf "chewing a stalk of garlic" would not
leave him to his privacy, just as there are always thousands of
such oafs who do not participate in or understand the higher com-
munings and presumed purposes of their rulers. Ulysses warns
him explicitly: "Stranger . . . I have sailed to all lands, / killed
in all lands, and come home poor. I think / blood buys nothing,
and I think it buys / all that's bought." The oaf stays. Ulysses
prays to heaven for guidance, and gets none. When the fool
"raises his staff against me," Ulysses explains he "halved him like
a melon!" He describes the ease of the blow that did it, certain
what to do but uncertain what it meant: "Was it my life / or the
god's laughter answered?" His situation is not mitigated. In anger
and disrespect at what the gods seem to be demanding of him, he
tosses the body into his sacrificial fire, then, one by one, the dead
man's herd of goats. Doubting the wisdom of the gods yet not
their existence, Ulysses still obeys the hieratic forms of his
religion, though the substance with which he has filled the forms
is repugnant to him. Darkness has come by the end of the blood
bath. He has lost his road, slept, and awakened near a temple to
Apollo, "But across his belly / a crack grinned hip to hip, and the
right hand / lay palm-up in the dust." It was the first of many
such "cracked gods" and "dusty altars" he came across. In his last
reflection before the end, he concludes that " . . . the
memory / could not live in the fact. I had grown old / in the

wrong world." That is, he had lived by one set of values while the facts supported another. Penelope had woven for nothing in that same wrong world. "I could not return," he realizes, for "I was woven to my dead men." The ending is ambiguous:

> In the dust
> of the dead shore by the dead sea I lay down
> and named their names who had matched lives with me,
> and won. And they were all I loved. (56)

Presumably, the names are those who had been his comrades. In what way had they won, other than dying still convinced of their purpose and cause, their illusions intact? They died in that "wrong world" which was still "right" to them. Why were they all he loved? Because of their contending with him in a cause, or because they died with their illusions? But suppose those who matched lives with him were the various persons he had killed while he was in his state of illusion. He could love them just as well; or more, perhaps, in that they gave him the tangible proof that he was acting under the aegis of the gods.

Ulysses is like many a character in Ciardi's poems, not unlike the young airman Ciardi himself was, in his case saved by his sense of humor and gift of poetry. Ulysses comes to knowledge of himself in relation to the ultimates he has lived by. The knowledge is almost more than he can bear. He has lost his religion, his faith in the gods and their purpose for him. He is more utterly alone than any man should be. In this respect, he is like the marooned man, whose immediate plight was only physical, in "Man Stranded" from *Homeward to America*. We are left with a haunting sense of incompleteness, of betrayal, like the survivor of twenty years earlier, like other Ciardi characters. What then must be done now? Whatever it is, we must decide it and then do it for ourselves. Ciardi will make specific and reiterate that point in future poems.

Somewhat surprisingly, the poems about artists in *39 Poems* are not among their author's best work. (The same thing could be said of most of his brief essays, often obituary notices, on poets, when compared to his other essays.) They seem to be exercises of wit and not necessary poems. They sometimes seem blown up with a quality of not-so-fine excess, by sheer determination, from a kernel of genuine response. Thus they do not always seem genuine. When they do not, it is often because they imitate their nominal subject. This is the worst that can be said of them. There are poems to Lorca, Dylan Thomas, Ezra Pound, Jacques Lipchitz, Wallace Stevens, Winfield Townley Scott, and Richard Eberhart. "Some Figures for Who Must Speak" is a poem in several parts about approaches to art and their relations to life. Whatever occasions provoked these poems, one must note there are many poets and artists whom Ciardi has responded to yet who are not here. The point is to suggest that, even in these relative failures, Ciardi made an effort to write real poems about aspects of art and not just to try his hand at pastiche or to write charmingly or otherwise to personal friends, as Winfield Townley Scott and Richard Eberhart were.

The "Homage to Lorca" in *39 Poems*, for example, begins with four lines of Spanish as an epigraph, meaning, roughly "You were alive, my God, inside the monstrance piercing your Father with needles of light. Pulsing like the poor heart of the frog that the doctors put in the test tube." Ciardi's poem is built around these images. As so often, he uses the hieratic references of a Christianity that neither he nor the subject of his homage espoused into their maturity. Thus the poem can easily seem a puffed-up, rhetorical exercise unless the imagery redeem it. The central image is the ". . . frog's heart in the monstrance, / beating the specimen day of scientist Christ; as in a ray of light. . . ." Lorca the man, the poet, the symbol—none is really as important as exploiting the images. At its worst, the poem seems not so much insincere as inauthentic. What to make of this death? "Fact, says the song of the dead man," and the poet has "no duty to say more." Confined to the world of fact, "The song does not transcend but signify / the fact of the man." And that overriding fact is that he is dead. The murdered poet's body proclaimed that "man's mystery is to sweeten his own death." This seems to be the American poet's humanistic point that man must create his own values and perform them sufficiently if his death is to have meaning before the immense but monstrous nothingness of Death and in relation to the life the survivors continue with. The poet's work, his life, his death affirm life all the way from a frog's heart kept alive in a test tube by doctors through the range of the human experience of life: "Give, says the song of the dead man. Touch. Feel." The poem brings together Ciardi's affirmation of life and art, and Lorca is the incidental means to bear the American poet's recurrent themes. This same thing is generally true of the other artist poems. But this point included the additional one that in the midst of a diversity of subjects and approaches, Ciardi has recurrent concerns and values. He comes back to the same points over and again; he finds them in nearly every subject. "Finds" should be emphasized here. The points are not forced on the subjects. If this is a way to point to the limits of the poet, it is equally a way to point to his strengths and his value for his readers. Testing his own experiences, he tests ours, too. We can walk a little way in the darkness, at least, aided by his light. If the light does not illuminate the bottom of the well, what light does? One would not want to be without this poet's light.

"Some Figures for Who Must Speak" takes Ciardi's deep-held conviction, the faith in the significance and worth of the "as if" world of art, and poses against it the difficulties art has in achieving reconciliation because of human subjectivity whether it is simply innate or culturally shaped. The poem in six parts exists in a mythical realm in which time is obliterated. The narrator is on the one hand a primitive huntsman; on the other, he discusses poetry with a Baptist graduate student in Florida. As he says, though, "this is all times and all scenes," and claims to "speak for the family in all its ages." Poetry in this context is "the family talk of the generations." The poem takes the form of a negotiation between representatives of hostile tribesmen. The effort is to express something marvelous out of the essential experience of the life of the tribe, imaged as a white elk. This figure seems to correspond to the marvelous qualities in the experience of life, if they could only be seen that way. The narrator claims true perception for himself, but still "cannot name it / by any names you know." The sign of this difficulty of communication he illustrates by responses to the word "Poetry": the second-person "you" thinks of Longfellow while the first thinks "of the race in its going: the family at its days: / the young at the edge of the thicket where the elk sleeps." The poem is not really successful; yet it has a duality that is Ciardi's own. Men seek the same ultimate goals, for which no single name can be found. In conceiving the quest and seeking what they conceive, they define their own nature, which is really a definition of all men as well. Poetry has the capacity to bridge the differences between individual and group definitions, if people could see it truly; but the same difficulties pertain. So men remain together yet apart—and to each adjective may be affixed "in their humanity."

The dustjacket of *39 Poems* included two paragraphs by Ciardi making another comment on his book. Addressing the reader, the poet wants him to "find a voice" in the poems and hopes "the voice will be worth letting into your head." If this volume is less than one of the indispensable books of the modern age, it is at least the record of a voice in a given age, more or less how the age seemed to a contemporary, and very much worth letting into one's head. What it has to say runs through all of Ciardi's work, but if one reads for theme only rather than the experience, he does not like poetry in the first place. The thirty-nine poems are "Unimportant" like most of Ciardi's poems, but to the right reader they offer such immemorial themes as love of family, love of life, faith in the durability of art, a contempt for merely material values, and others, all refracted through the wit and sensibility of a very modern American circa 1959, and finding outlet in a number of accomplished poems. Many a fashionable book has done a great deal less.

II   In the Stoneworks *(1961)*

The poems of *In the Stoneworks* indicate that Ciardi is on a plateau of accomplishment. Though the publisher's dustjacket blurb claims "new horizons" for the poet, there is nothing in the volume that shows any advance beyond *39 Poems*. No poem here would have seemed out of place in the previous three volumes, save for thematic groupings. In its forty-eight poems, divided into three sections of twenty, fourteen, and fourteen, there is a great variety, including several more or less conventional poems, some narratives, and many that show Ciardi's humanistic, affirmative yet ironic values. No single poem is really outstanding; a few are trivial, and one or two may be failures. None is really intense or complicated. Some of these things could be construed as the ease of manner of a poet who is the master of his methods and often chooses to present himself in a relaxed or casual style. "Song " reminds one of Frost's "The Need of Being Versed in Country Things," despite its different references, in the uncomprehending indifference of nature to the affairs of men. Auden's "Epilogue" is recalled in the mannerism of "Dialogue," "Tick," and especially in "A Dialogue in the Shade," but the first and third of these look forward to the greater achievement of "Tenzone," a dialogue of body and soul in *Person to Person*. The father poem, "It Took Four Flowerboats to Convoy My Father's Black," adds new details to the legend of the father's death but is not one of the poet's better works on the subject. "It Is Spring, Darling" is a love poem, quieter than many in *I Marry You*, where the bullyboy as successful lover *is* somewhat noisy. It seems under the inspiration of Dylan Thomas's "When All My Five and Country Senses See" for its central consideration of the five senses.

The poem that gives its title to the book seems to be set where "S.P.Q.R." (*39 Poems*) was set but to have more general implications. Instead of Rome as such, this one is "In the stoneworks under God," but with the same broken statuary of deities slowly weathering back to their elements. The same process in time will make "even the stoneworks / under the stoneworks stand bare to the unmade day."[6] Even nature must undergo the process of which man is the most interesting respondent. Insofar as the poem represents the common denominator of all things, it becomes a suitably comprehensive abstraction for the title of the volume.

Perhaps the really significant thing, which is no more than a matter of emphasis, is that the poems are more generalized and therefore less personal than earlier. Even when Ciardi writes a love poem, such as "Song for an Allegorical Play," one of his best, what we know of the author, his wife, his marriage, and the like is neither a necessary factor nor an obstacle in our response. This may mean that the poems are less passionately emotional than other more personal poems, but perhaps they are only less specifically personal, for they remain recognizably Ciardi's. His ideas, his themes, his references, his diction, his movement through a poem are all recognizably present. If the mode of the poems is less that of personal, individual emotion, it is the more that of thoughtful reflection.

The first section, best of the three, is called "Back Home in Pompeii," after one of the poems. A native of the lost city narrates, by means of selected details, the end, in which he perished. He is amazed at the artifacts and replicas, when

> Storms later, we awoke
> and strolled among ourselves
> in the excavated bed—
> stone castings on stone shelves. (5)

His conclusion, though lightly put, is an important one for Ciardi:

Well, that's that.
Settled down
and starting to get fat
in another town
oceans away,
we only come to see
a curiosity
on holiday. (6)

The Pompeians are no different from any other people. Human
beings are the same for the whole time of man, and two thousand
years have made no difference in them. This means that not only
can one plumb one's own depths and still say something pertinent
for others, one's contemporaries, but also that one can draw examples anywhere in the past, interpret them as one does oneself
and one's contemporaries, and be both historically accurate and
pertinent to present and future. Slight as the poem is, it shows for
certain that Ciardi now has grand dimensions to work with.
Possibly the study and translation of Dante have aided him in this
respect.

Awareness of this unity of mankind is necessary to read properly "In the Garden of the Hurricane's Eye," a poem about Adam
and Eve, for it provides a better reading than does looking for
allegory or parable. It is easier to be ponderous than not on such a
subject or, escaping that, to be coy. Ciardi avoids both adroitly.
The primal pair seem doomed to gain no more than knowledge of
their own natures; the sexual aspects are set forth in some detail.
The only mention of a serpent appears to be most immediately
Adam's sexual organ: "Out of its ripped roots rose the blood-
webbed snake." The couple find more than satisfaction in
themselves. Each finds sufficiency and definition in the other.
Angels, "God's birds," have come in a ship in difficult weather.
Adam rejects their help. For Eve, he works in burning drought to
salvage what he could of "spoiled fruits," and "dug roots / and
brought them to her." The purity of the angels is marked by
Adam's blood from a gashed arm that stains one sail of the boat.
Eve kisses the half-healed wound of the sleeping Adam, first in
tenderness and then in "a sobbing passion," which starts the
blood again. In pain he calls her name, "Eve," presumably for
the first time, and then they sate their sexual passion. Eve knew
his name for the first time and said it over to herself silently. Here

is their human definition, including names, their turning to each other in pain and passion; yet this definition is not entire:

> "How dark he is," she thought, "even the moon
> leaves him half shadowy." But when she lay
> beside him, she, too, darkened and went out.
>
> Then a branch moved, and both of them lay lit. (13)

For all that is mysterious in their attraction, that is dark in their separate identities, the acceptance of their necessity to be together, whether understood or not, transfigures all darkness into any light there is. Confronting the captain of the angels before they depart and seeing his own blood on their sail, Adam smiled. At this point, Adam gains his ultimate knowledge:

> He saw Him then: an eye in his mind's eye,
> a calm raged found by storms. And at the center?
> Was that it? to be locked in calm, but powerless
> to calm what raged? To pity God the lusts
> that hurled Him round, yet kept their distance from Him? (14)

Adam has one last choice. The Angel has orders to drive him from the Garden, to which Adam responds: "It was His eye moved and let in / the rage around it. Now, what garden is there / but what I make myself?" Confronting the question of whether to go with the angels or to stay, Adam feeling "his first power" asks, "Has He a garden not ringed round by rages?" His conclusion is not that he stay in the Garden or another one, but that the Angel go away and leave him to his own devices. Adam's decision was not made entirely out of concern for Eve; she is part but not all. His own stubborn independence is important. The departing Angel gives Adam "a burning branch." Alone, he turns and there is Eve risen from her hiding place, "And waved. And the branch burned." The poem ends. Anything else is up to Adam and Eve, left with themselves and a token of light and warmth from an unknown God as a symbol. In a striking narrative, Ciardi reiterates and affirms his humanistic values, which are never simple and in this guise have nothing of the sentimental. That ability with narrative, shown in every book, is not the least considerable quality of the poem. It will find its fullest fruition in the *Lives of X*.

If the Adam and Eve poem brings the primal pair down to grand but still human dimensions, the more usual Ciardi approach, which has already been noted several times, appears in the family poem, always a fruitful subject for this poet.

"Bedlam Revisited" is based on episodes from the author's childhood which are also used in *Lives of X* and elsewhere. This poem is superior because, though it generalizes the experience, it does not require the personal intervention of the author; rather, keeping to historical facts, it manages to lift the events to a larger suggestiveness. He describes vividly the details of his early childhood in a Boston slum, "four families to a john." Though he came out hating "the Boss, the Cop and the Ghost of / the Irish Trinity," still it took place "in a happy reek of garlic, bay, and clove." Nobody told him anything much because "Nobody had / anything much to tell me." How could the child know that "everything about us was full-moon mad? / Or that I'd find few saner? It wasn't bad." The understated explanation of this line is the triumph of the poem. This is the meaning one got from the experience; this is an analogue for all one ever gets for the meaning of life:

> Someone always answered the telephone
> when it had rung too long. You got only a tone
> when they finally called you—far away and sad.
> But it didn't matter. There would have been nothing to say.
> Later they changed the number and we moved away. (21)

Ciardi himself picked "Song for an Allegorical Play" for inclusion in *Poet's Choice*, edited by Paul Engle and Joseph Langland, to represent his work at its best. In his commentary, he describes it as his "best love poem": "It sings me an image, an idea, and a tone I'd like to live by and to keep my loves by." Yet it has an impersonal quality that would have seemed out of place in *I Marry You*. Though his commentary says little about the poem, it does bring out that he likes "both poems that sing and poems that say. Singing and saying both have their rhythms, and any good rhythm is a joy to find. Basically, I think, I am a 'saying' poet. Perhaps I like this Song because it feels successful as a singing poem. How can one fail to be happy about singing?" He adds that the poem is "in my own voice" and, in explanation of the title, "in a voice that would do for a play," a poetical play he might someday write but which he can explain no better than as an " 'allegorical enactment.' "[7]

The poem puts in opposition two qualities in each person, represented by a church mouse and a wart hog. The former stands for "our scraping small decay," the latter for "the gross jowls of flesh on bone." Love in its most compassionate form is called here "mercy." The recurrent term "mercy" Ciardi once defined as an "exchange of needs."[8]

The first stanza is a fervent wish that lovers (first person plural), in the name of love, could rise "paunch from paunch . . . / false and unmartyred, to pretend / we dress for Heaven in the end," with the church mouse forgiven and the wart hog acknowledged. The second stanza elaborates and justifies the wish. If the lovers were able to look, accept, and admit their qualities, "think what a sweetness tears might be / in mercy, each by each set free." "Each by each" most immediately refers to the tears, but also should refer to the mouse and the wart hog, and further to the lovers set free of the encumbrances of these qualities. A playful sense of paradox dominates the last two stanzas. What is the "Success" of "Only Success is beast enough / to stop our hearts"? Presumably, it would be success if each lover were to rid himself of the failings of church mouse and wart hog, but that would stop their hearts from loving. So, with a paradox worthy of Donne or Marvell,

> When best we love
> we have no reason but to fail,
> in reason learning as we live
> we cannot fail what we forgive. (9)

Love is beyond reason, and it is reason to acknowledge this fact. In loving at their best, if the achievement may not be Success with a capital S, nevertheless they "cannot fail" the things that are forgiven in love. The mouse that will take crumbs and the wart hog that would devour everything, respectively, are in the eyes and blood of both lovers. If they are able to accept each other's qualities in compassionate love, then "all our queer beasts" will be understood, shall be transformed into something admirable "and be, / in mercy, each by each set free." Here, it is the beasts that will be set free in mutuality. The paradox is that the lovers cannot love without the qualities of church mouse and wart hog each has, yet love at its height could set the beasts free. The poem gains from being read in the context of other Ciardi poems. Seen there, it has his typical qualities, is in his "own voice." These are irony at the expense of human nature which is deplorable, yet the paradox that those very qualities are the source of the best that man is capable of and thus a means to affirm man and the duality of his condition.

There are several kinds of poems in the section "Voices," most of them adequate. "Launcelot in Hell" is a revisionist account of the legendary love affair and its aftermath, told by Launcelot himself. He fought and killed Arthur. He is a manly fellow, and, though not an oaf, he is a long way from the Victorian sentimentalist Tennyson portrayed. To him, Guinevere is "the best mare ever danced on turf. . . ." Arthur "couldn't sit *that* saddle," but Launcelot "rode her: / king's mount from bell to cockcrow while bed, castle, and country / shook under us. . . ." He took his "damnation as it came and would have hacked / a thousand Arthurs small to mount her again." Badly wounded in the battle that left the country in ruins and eight thousand of the best men in England dead, he rode out and never looked back—and thought of Guinevere. When he found her, he was outraged that she had become a nun, "A whore of heaven wailing / from a black cassock. . . ." This was the death of everything he had lived for, that "she dared not even look at what we were!" What is a manly fellow to do? This one, wrapped in his worldliness, "did not turn back," "did not look back" for the one with whom he had dared the world "beyond damnation":

> Should I turn now for a mare? Let Heaven ride her spavined:
> I had the heat of her once, and I'd sooner
> have turned Saracen and ripped the crosses from Europe
> than deny my blood spilled into his in the field that made us. (49)

Any man who would not have been "scorched" when "she danced like a flame" was dead anyway, "Dead as the clerk / who rhymed us to a moral. There is no moral. I was. He was. She was. / Blood is a war." His last thought is of Arthur, and here he sounds like Ciardi's Ulysses in *39 Poems*. Lancelot fought Arthur nearly to his own death, "And would again. Without her. Stroke for stroke. For his own sake. / Because no other iron dared me whole." Ciardi admires this kind of fellow.

The poems in "Natures" are a miscellaneous lot, on the whole lighter in tone and manner, though not necessarily less penetrating. "Faces" and "An Antarctic Hymn" will stand for all of them here. In the first the narrator, evidently Ciardi himself, once hitchhiked from Ann Arbor to Boston in the middle of December. In Canandaigua, the young man was given a ride in a Buick just after dark, the face in shadow behind the voice which invited, " 'Jump in,' it said. 'It's cold.' " The driver with the never-seen face took him five miles out of town, let him out on the pretext of turning off, then turned around and headed back toward town, stopping only to say, "You haven't thanked me for the ride. . . ." Receiving a wary "Thanks," he added, "You're welcome, brother. Keep the rest for change." Just short of frostbite, he was picked up by a truck. The speculation that is the basis of the poem is what did that face look like?—"for twenty years / I've been finding faces that might do for his." Certainly, no facile optimist was haunted for twenty years by that experience.

"An Antarctic Hymn" in four rhymed quatrains tells the story, or rather, gives an example, like a preacher's illustration in a sermon, of a myopic preacher bringing the message to penguins that "mankind was loved." In their midst, "he stood counting souls to Paradise." The first-person narrator, in a secular metaphor but in an unspecified enterprise, was himself "holy once till I went damned / flush in the best hour of my hocus-pocus." He "dreamed of Heaven's Rose Bowl crammed," whereupon his undeluded vision returned. The rest of the poem is a mock-prayer to "Our Father Birdsong" to the effect that "Thy fox" be sent to scourge the floes of "waddling flocks / which neither sing nor fly, and pass as men / to squinty saints. . . ." The reason is that no one, "for mercy," shall be deluded to think that the creatures have souls or that any do "but that they sing and lift." The saint will "die of joy" in the assumption that the empty floes mean the souls have gone to Paradise. The prayer includes the wish that "rancid red, / Thy fox burn over him on the last drift." The image presents a problem. The fox was asked for to keep the saint from the delusion of his good intentions which the narrator has been disabused of earlier. But the saint will not be disabused in his extremity and perishes in delusion at what was meant as succor. That being true, the fox, his purpose misunderstood, is now "rancid red," but still an ambiguous agent of good intentions. Is the

fox at the last a protector of the unsavable saint in his delusion?
And what of the narrator in whose prayer the fox exists in the first
place? No matter how simply it begins, any Ciardi poem is apt to
turn into a complex of ironic interrelationships that probe deep
into human experience.

III   In Fact (1962)

This volume is trivial, the weakest in the Ciardi canon. There is
hardly a good poem in it; this is to judge him against his own performance elsewhere. Sometimes a book can be weak because an
author is experimenting, going from one theme or manner to
another, and finally is vindicated when the transition is complete, but that is not the case here. *In Fact* represents something
Ciardi had long been able to do, a kind of *vers de société* or witty
light verse that illuminates a little but not much, that lifts a little
but not very high. Critics sometimes speak of an author mani-
festing an "assimilated technique" in his work (it has been said of
Ciardi), by which they seem to mean a technical facility that
leaves no rough edges showing, is adequate to any demands made
on it, and results in finished, more or less satisfactory, poems.
Ciardi has done these things in the fifty-four short poems of *In
Fact*. Yet something is missing. The perception is there, but no
great substance. He is not really involved—perhaps that is what
we miss, Ciardi himself. The wit is there, but it often takes the
form of mere verbal cleverness, and any illusion the poem creates
lasts no longer than a soap bubble. The subjects that are not such
fancies are mostly out of well-to-do suburban life. The book could
be construed in its weaknesses as exemplifying the qualities of this
subject, but Ciardi knows how to do better.

The critical response is interesting. Ciardi could make a living,
no doubt in part has made one, from the brief reviews of his
works in the *Library Journal* which serve as guides for acquisition
librarians. Most of their hundred-word comments on Ciardi's
books end with the advice "For all literature collections" that,
surely, has helped the books go into multiple printings. The
review of *In Fact* assumes that "few poets in America have a more
secure or popular reputation than John Ciardi. . . ." The logic
behind this assertion is that "certainly he is one of the most
human" of poets.[9] In general, on the above premises, the poet is
praised for his forthrightness, his honesty, and the variety of his

work; he is said to be like ourselves. These statements are not untrue and are in the line of the author's known intentions, but
what is missing is critical judgment. If Ciardi had not been an
editor of a prestigious middlebrow journal or a fixture of the college lecture circuit, would the comments have been different?
Would the poems have been published at all?

Judson Jerome and Richard Howard, two critics who are also
poets, make what cases can be made. And Miller Williams, also a
poet, chose eight poems from *In Fact* to include in his selection,
The Achievement of John Ciardi; only *From Time to Time* supplied as many for his selection that ranged through *This Strangest
Everything* (1966). Is the explanation taste or sympathy or
editorial necessity for the short poem?

Jerome's review, written for Ciardi's own journal, was
presumably assigned and approved by the poet himself. It begins
with the negative observation that *In Fact* is not what anyone
(least of all, he imagined, John Ciardi), would call "a great book
or even a particularly important one." He did find it "damned en-
joyable reading," which he deemed remarkable enough among
new books of poems. He saw it as a "day-by-day sort of book," in
which "None of the poems are particularly ambitious, as in
Ciardi's other volumes." He drew a comparison to the spirit of the
classical epigrams, but asked, "is it finally enough?" He knew the
answer is that no one said it was[10]—for any of us, certainly not for
Ciardi himself. It is just that if we are attuned to the full Ciardi
resonance, we miss the parts that are absent from *In Fact*, even if
we respond to the reedy strain we do get.

In Fact contains several love poems, but these, if occasionally
graceful, add nothing to the poet's achievement in this line. "As I
Would Wish You Birds" skirts popular-song sentimentality,
though in the cause of subjectivity and imagination which Ciardi
had long laid poetic claim to. Is it pseudoprofundity or cuteness?
"You never see Gulls in aviaries. Gulls are / distance. Who can
put distance in a cage?"[11] Gulls are Ciardi's birds. He has written
most convincingly about them of all birds. Here he does not serve
them well, despite his feeling for them. "In Pity as We Kiss and
Lie" is clever with its plays on "hardly right" and "softly true,"
"softly wrong" and "hardly wrong," as well as "lie and kiss" and
"kiss and lie" and variations. "By the Sea" picks up the idea
Ciardi expressed in his notice of *I Marry You* that death is the impetus to intensity in love. The theme is "had we world enough

and time," what would it matter? Marvell did it better in "To His Coy Mistress." The link between the title and the poem may be personal to the author, but no connection is made in the poem itself.

A poem that has the manner of these but without the obvious faults is "Of the Kingdom." "Love" and "mercy," both much-used terms in the poet's work, are closely related if not identical. Love can begin only if one will "let people be wrong," because justice in its sternness "will hang / all of us yet." When love comes in, mercy can go out, and "ah, then / a bird song may defend us, / a mote—can you dream it?—heal!"

There are successes in *In Fact*, but they are small by comparison to those of other books. "My Tribe" by using no metaphors becomes a large metaphor itself: "Everyone in my tribe hates / everyone in your tribe," and the narrator's group "shall all finally kick all of your / heads. We are united." This is ambiguous in its intentions. Ciardi is an advocate of a large sympathy and tolerance that grow out of personal forms of both. For example, his speaker in "Oration" voices something he approves, namely tearing up his passport and taking out "citizenship in the human race." But the poem on the tribe is a kind of analogue for every group united by worthy ideals which are narrow enough to be exclusive, narrow enough to cause the hatred of anything different from the letter of the faith.

In *Lives of X* this sort of thing is associated with the Catholicism of the Boston Irish. In *In Fact*, it is closer to WASP America, as in "Letter to a Wrong Child." That poem has no sense of inevitability, but of a forced existence hammered together by the poet. Martin Luther is responsible for a kind of neurotic anxiety-state that makes self-forgiveness for a human past both necessary and almost impossible. If psychiatry will not suffice, the poem advises, then travel to some of the poorer parts of the world for a remedy. The travel should not just be made to move around but to encounter realms of experience that are outside the awareness of well-to-do America. Naples is held up

> not as a place but as an
> overpopulated idea; as a self-loving,
> self-seeking, self-murdering, self-
> demonstrating disarrangement and
> sequences of ideas made up of too many
> other ideas called, sometimes, lives. (67)

Tracing that "city-as-idea" back to "its first blood" is enough to bring about the desired self-forgiveness, or else one is a hopeless case and suicide is then permitted by a bullet through an "otherwise impenetrable head. . . ." It is only in the last lines that the nominative of address is explicit: "my martyr, my poor, alas, white / protestant middle-class wept goose / of this prosperous wrong paved / barnyard." The "letter" is signed "With love. / Father." The general intent of the poem is clearer than some of its details. The poem has a certain power, but as an instructor of the nation Ciardi is less than effective. When he preaches the doctrine of himself and by implication and analogy the rest of us, he has a chance to succeed with the presented experience or message or whatever. But in "Letter to a Wrong Child" he is preaching from the outside to the rest of us, even if in the person of "Father." His proper place is "in ego with us all," but he seems outside, to the mitigation of the emotional force of the poem. It will not finally work on the terms presented to us.

The poems of *In Fact* are closer in many ways to Ciardi's "Manner of Speaking" columns for the *Saturday Review* than to his earlier poetry. He has turned many a nice column on the foibles of well-to-do but poor, educated but ignorant, well-intentioned but racially-prejudiced middle-class America. Given the author's other poems, there is no reason to think the columns have really affected his poetry, especially as the next volume is the generally excellent *Person to Person*. The poems of *In Fact* are like little diary entries, and the year was not a notable one.

IV   Person to Person *(1964)*

In this volume of fifty-seven poems Ciardi strikes out in no new directions as to theme or form, but maintains a high level of competence with what he has already marked out as his own. The manner is relaxed in tone, but not the form or the control of the elements of the poems. It would not be a Ciardi book without personal poems, and here they seem to achieve a kind of generality in which readers can find their own meanings as well as his. His long-standing contention about art is that it should provide this possibility, though here it seems to be achieved by a relaxed ease rather than by intense deep-plunging. He does at last, however, after stating his own truths accurately, achieve a more general significance through the pronounced use of analogy.

The method used for most of these poems is the quite traditional one of giving a description of a scene or an object, carrying through a small action if only of the mind's response, and concluding with a generalization, interpretation, or attributed meaning which opens out still wider in its implications. The circles widen on the "rippling pools "(to use his phrase from *How Does a Poem Mean?* for the expanding circles of meaning a poem can have). The method is associated especially with Robert Frost in poems like "Stopping by Woods on a Snowy Evening," "Birches," and many others. Some of Ciardi's lines actually sound Frostean, both in the meditative cast, the rhymes, and the pattern of pauses: "Some rule of birds kills off the song / in any that begin to grow / much larger than a fist or so" ("The Size of Song"); and also: "And still I look at this / world as world's will be seen—in what light there is" ("Sea Marshes in Winter")[12] and others. But, of course, however much the manner is associated with Frost, no poet can claim exclusive rights to a method as general as analogy. It is reasonable to think that Ciardi was "influenced" by Frost, as in the past by other poets. There is no doubt of the younger poet's admiration for the older, and in the past he had tried the manner of admired poets' works for himself, as though still exploring the possibilities of the many first-personal singulars he is. Still, the poems are Ciardi's. Frost would not have written them in quite this way. They are their author's own work in virtues and faults, and little or nothing is new in either category.

"The Size of Song" is about the songs of birds, meditated as an abstraction. If since the Romantics a bird's song is a symbol of the poet's art, here the ripples widen to much more than that. In two stanzas of eight lines, with definite rhymes, we move from the phenomenon that, as rule one, the bigger the bird the less the song, and the suggestive conclusion that "Birds let us know / the songsters never are the strong"; on to rule two, that the largest birds cannot fly either, and the general application: "Give up the skies: / you're left your weight. And your last ties / to anything that sings." The sky is another conventional Romantic symbol for aspiration, effort, imagination, the beyond, perspective, and the like. Relinquish the one, the reader is urged, and he is left with the physical, representative of the gross, earthbound, nonvocal, nonexpressive state. One recalls, too, Ciardi's remark that basically he is a saying rather than the singing poet. What he says here, in a manner between the two, is a suggestive statement about the nature of singing and any endeavor that fits the pattern.

What Ciardi can do with visual images alone—and he is especially effective in visual effects—can be seen in "Gulls Land and Cease to Be." He uses ten rhymed lines in a pattern that, with variations, is a favorite of his: ababcdcdee. The title adds a suggestion of interpretation to what is otherwise pure description. In "ceasing to be," the gulls cease to be themselves in their essence, which is motion and distance. As we have seen, gulls are the birds that provoke Ciardi most among the feathered host. The mere presentation of images is too limiting a thing for this poet to write other than occasionally. He is restless, uncomfortable with a given world as it is; he is after significance, meaning. He seeks the contradictions a man perceives, the human, his own response, what the mind can make of experience. He wants ideas, perspectives, as, for example, if there were gulls in Eden. He wants connections, similitudes. Nature offers him no reading of the spirit, only an occasional illustration or analogy or provocation.

One of the best poems of the book, for example, "Tree Trimming," is a family poem that offers no philosophical musings at all. The language is straightforward, colloquial, and profound. It uses the method of analogy, but the poet makes the connection explicitly and develops it. Doing the unfamiliar work of climbing a tree to trim its limbs, the poet is reminded by his tiredness and sweating "who my people were." What better way than this to "say my father's or my grandfather's name. . ."? He concentrates the poem on this immediate family, as far back as his knowledge goes, but surely the whole of Adam's wages is suggested. He is aware that his condition is but a semblance, their experience profounder of what he has only touched, the "green growing / and the dirt under it and the day going." They had what he can never have:

> They had first things and the power
> and the ignorance that go to the receiver
> of first things only; that and no more.
>
> I've lost it. I'm my own first. (9)

The poet with his education, including languages, and his sporadic practice of what they were committed fully to, realizes that even his father, who "did read some" approached things from the personal and the local: ". . . it was / his mountain he came from, not the mind / of man. He had ritual, not ideas." Reverence he had, presumably, rather than idea and the consciousness of idea. The sense of deracination that so haunts modern intellectuals is poignantly expressed. The problem is complicated by the fact that the poet has children. He can sense the immemorial human condition and identity of his forebears in the person of his father, "But he is / more than I can teach my children. They / have no first life." Here is the plight of that well-to-do middle-class America he tried to instruct in "Letter to a Wrong Child" and seemed superior to in several poems of *In Fact*. The point is to show not an inconsistency or contradiction in Ciardi (though he is many men, as he has pointed out) but that he is one in his humanity with his fellow contemporaries, even if committed by the requirements of certain poems to take partial views of their plight. The poet's children, starting from the material but not the spiritual point to which he has attained, have lost the important links with the past; they could work and sweat and feel only tired. The poet wishes poignantly for an identity for his children, which he owns dimly and they not at all:

> I wish we were Jews and could say
> the names of what made us.
> I could weep by slow waters for my son
> who has no history, no name
> he knows long, no ritual from which he came,
> and no fathers but the forgotten. (10)

This poem is not really a sign of discord in the poet's own family, the rock on which he has built his bastion. He could say at this point to the memoryless son, "I love you," just as he could later, when one of his sons was arrested for the third or fourth time for a marijuana violation, in *The Little That Is All*. But he is too perceptive not to be aware of the differences and too much a poet not to be able to give the perception a form. We get a little paradigm of America, at least, in the move from the traditionalist to the self-made man to the deracinated modern with the implications of this cycle for the future. In a plain style that is almost devoid of metaphor and is entirely devoid of ornament, Ciardi has written a poem of power, emotional appeal, and significance.

The heart of *Person to Person* is the second section of twenty-five poems; it gives its title to the book and takes its title from a poem of that name. If the method of analogy is applied in the reading, this poem is a fitting one to characterize the entire book. Though it is not one of the really fine ones but rather in the middle register with its ironies good-humored, its laughter is as profound as fate. The poem indicates a pattern of the difficulty of communication from any person to any others, or to any vital connection, using the jargon of the telephone operators. The poet's difficulty in reaching his readers or hearers is only one of the circles of this rippling pool. "No one / see-ums to ants-err," the disembodied voice reports. This is Ciardi's version of a perennial quest for certainty, not too far removed from the idea in George Meredith's "What a dusty answer gets the soul when hot for certainty in this our life," yet remote in another world entirely in its language from our bustling technological world. As part of the poet's effort to communicate "person to person," Ciardi makes explicit the link with ultimates. We are all in this together and know the voice "from fate," the presumed human source of which we never see. It is like life, yet different, "blurred," "much as an over-used die goes on stamping parts / with its worn intaglios." Though the results are not precisely what are wanted, still they almost suffice, they "will do," in fact "will have to do. We have the way we all live." And yet—and yet! The narrator "could be some sweetheart's / hope about to say it all." He could equally be "man's own last word / waiting to be gasped," or on a more mundane and inclusive level only the weather report, but not negligible since everybody's picnic depends upon it. The largest aspect is given as an off-handed concession, a charming application of the "as if" approach. If we assume the disembodied voice has a corporeal residence, it "might as readily be swiveled to the switchboard / / of Heaven, melodious to this world's need, plugging in / tears, prayers, and praises, each to its office." The poem comes deliberately back down to the routine of human existence after establishing the larger analogy. When the connection is not made, the narrator suffers a "non-death," he can "reach no one." With a terse "Thank you," he goes "under the ether of failure. Not dead, no. But missing and amiss."

The two most notable poems of this section of *Person to Person* are "Autobiography of a Comedian" and "Tenzone." The first is a successful application of the "person to person" principle. In running over the details of his own life, Ciardi poses them in such a way that the conclusion is valid—certainly it is thought-provoking, if anyone demur at its validity—for all of us. This poem, too, in the context of Ciardi's work looks forward to the extended treatment of the author's life to be found in *Lives of X*, and especially the attitudes expressed in "Letter to an Indolent Norn." "Autobiography" is in sixteen rhymed quatrains, each stanza picking up one rhyme from the previous stanza, the rhymes often approximate. The first stanza rhymes abcb, the second dbab (if "embrace" is an approximate rhyme for "adolescence"), the third efdf, the fourth gfhf, and so on. The rhythm is basically iambic but varied, conversational, easygoing but sufficient to its purposes.

For all of its ease of utterance, the poem compresses a great deal of experience into a few lines. The details are familiar to any reader of Ciardi, if posed in a slightly different way. The poem begins in "the insanities of adolescence," the mother mad, the dead father still speaking to the future poet, the life-denying aspects of Christianity prominent above the boy's religious efforts ("the cross was bloody on the One Hill"). He wrestled with God awake and in tormenting nightmares until "there was nothing to do but die or embrace / a more comic spirit." He did the latter, to the horror of his family, who kept him sequestered from his friends, and of the parish priest, who used him as subject for preachments from the pulpit. With the tolerance of a past long reconciled, the poet can add, "—God knows he had more than enough to deplore." The next stage in the comedian's career was to turn his talents with language to money, presented in the metaphor of a dancer and juggler. Money, cars, and houses accrued, as he "grew rich grinning." Especially important, as we know from other poems, "Bankers learned to pronounce my name." He won at gambling in Harold's Club, evidently a remarkable thing to happen. He is "still winning / what I have no real use for but / might as well take." Age is not even thinning his hair. The step to the larger world is, "I tell you this world's as crazy as I was once," and a sign is that "Even scholars take me seriously." In the manner of the dramatic monologue though with the reader presumably as the auditor, the comedian anticipates the response of disbelief at his complaint and answers it with one of his recurrent qualities: "Friend, I am trying / as simple and as marvelous a thing as honesty." Elaborating, "I think we are of some Stone Age, you and I," and "How do we make sense of ourselves?" The only way he can make any sense of "presidents, popes, kings, / ministers, marshals, or policemen" is to "see the ritual featherings of the tribes in their hair." He recalls the time twenty years back when he was a "gunner for our tribe," but not "the invisible people" he helped to kill; the fires, not the things that burned.

It is not cynicism but irony, the fiction of the poem true in its "as if" world but not the personal credo of Ciardi the man, that results in the statement that Harold the gambler, now crazy for the conventional God, "has our real / mystery in his spinning department store. / What we all pray to is the dice, the wheel, / and the holy jackpot." Old ladies stand prayerful before slot machines waiting for an answer to their reverence, for "It's God they feel / coming at the next click." Harold gets an assured three percent cut from the house winnings. The narrator sees him as "Another / comic spirit," who, however, is as committed to gambling as an old grandmother involved in the hocus pocus of superstition. But the narrator sees no reason to believe (in the sense of have faith in) "what there is a sure three per cent of."

Surely, the poet views himself as representative of modern America in its fortuitous but ambiguous affluence, as he stands between "our slapstick successes" and "our wry confessions." The poem from this point in the penultimate stanza to the end is no longer in the first-person singular but the first-person plural. "This world" is set in Reno, which is presumably a symbol for the vision of modern life set forth in the poem. The low sea is to the west, and the high desert is to the east. In between is a kind of percipience designated as "the mercy that sees and knows why / we must not love ourselves too much— / though, having no other, we must, somehow, try."

Here is the typical Ciardi position toward himself, toward modern life, toward life itself. The quintessence of Ciardi's subjects, his attitudes, and his values, is to be found in "Autobiography of a Comedian," but at the same time the truth is the truth of art and not the full, literal truth to the man in person. The proof is not to be found in the poet's personal utterances, such as interviews and the like, though it is present there, but in the fact that other poems say other things, with different emphases, that may not be entirely reconcilable. Given the poem-by-poem approach Ciardi has of a mind and sensibility coming to terms as best it can with what provokes it, any inconsistency becomes a positive virtue. If poetry invariably stemmed from a staunch and closely reasoned philosophical or theological position, matters might be otherwise; but such is not the case, not with modern poets in general, and certainly not with Ciardi.

The other really notable poem of the "person to person" section of *Person to Person* is "Tenzone." The title is the first problem. *The Princeton Encyclopedia of Poetry and Poetics* defines the term as an "amoebean type of poetic composition" originating in early twelfth century Provence, whence it was carried to Italy, where it became common among "the poets of the *dolce stil nuovo*, including Dante." Its qualities are variable as to form, but contain a "verbal exchange" often in the form of invective, which, however, may not be personal. Seemingly, it would fit any subject so long as it was susceptible to satiric or similar response in the language of invective, but it could be imaginary with the "original argument and exchange . . . by the same person."[13] The definition did not relate the form to the dialogue of body and soul, though that seems a natural outlet for the qualities named. It was at least the application Ciardi made of it. The comparative looseness of the form, the strong language, the dramatic tension that allows one speaker to take both sides, the link with Italy and Dante are features enough to make it right for Ciardi. His poem, written in awareness of Yeats's "A Dialogue of Self and Soul," features six-line stanzas rhymed, roughly, ababcc and so on through five stanzas of an address of "Soul to Body," and five of a rejoinder from "Body to Soul." The poem is more or less an ironic self-appraisal of Ciardi himself, though it cuts both ways. Soul is rather smug, characterizing the duality that is body as well as himself as "That affable, vital, inspired even, and well-paid / persuader of sensibility with the witty asides . . ." and adding smugly "but, at core, lucent and unswayed— / a gem of serenest ray—" and claims in addition that he is "the well-known poet, critic, editor, and middle-high / aesthete of the circuit . . ." and then adds an "alas." When Body comes back in stanza six, he characterizes the same duality in a point by point, grammatically parallel rejoinder as "That grave, secretive, aspirant even, and bang-kneed / eternalist of boneyards with the swallowed tongue" and adds sarcastically, "but, at dream source, flaming and fire-freed— / a monk of dark-celled rays—" and then for the respectable categories of the first offers "heretic, ignorant, Jesuit, and who- / knows-what skeleton," followed by the insistence on the doubleness, for he "is, alas, not wholly you." The irony in these two stanzas is nicely balanced because the terms posed by each are double, both repulsive and something to be proud of. Each urges it as part of the other but acknowledges his own part in it.

Soul continues his characterization in terms of responses from the public. Various opinions are given about the poet's career, ranging from a wasted talent to none in the first place. Soul has contempt for the material and for any earthly pomp, such as the Cadillac, the fleshpot indulgences of "his home away from home / where the dolls are," which the poet likes. The objection is that the indulgences add nothing to his stature as poet. He is "a greedy pig" who wants everything and more besides: "cash, bourbon, his whim away from whom. / He's a belly, a wallet, a suit, a no-score / of the soul." Still presumably thinking of his own values, Soul says the poet is a failure at whatever he tries; actually, he uses rather unSoulful language in saying it "is a bust." He cannot do soulful contemplation because stillness "grinds / against the jitter in him and dies." Though he "gabs" about poetry, his practice merely "dabbles" at it like a hobby "in between serious pitches / for cash, free-loading, and the more expensive bitches." Waxing heated and eloquent in invective, Soul gives up on him (the duality that is the person). Here, put parenthetically, is the single crux in the poem, for at this point comes: "(And so say I.)." In a brief *Explicator* piece, Edward J. Gallagher offered the interpretation that it "is a responsive outburst by the Body to the Soul's climactic assertion of disavowal."[14] Since it makes no sense for Soul to emphasize his point in that way, the only other possible interpretation is that the poet himself breaks in; but the form does not call for such intrusion. Either way, the point would be to disavow the picture just painted. The Soul's invective, while making the traditional points against the unreality of the temporal and the physical ("He lives the way he lives as if it were real"), puts his complaints in a strangely coarse contemporary jargon. The successful poet, he continues to charge, is "A con man. A half truth. A swindler in the clear." The ultimate charge is, "He actually likes it here!"

The body comes back in terms as strong. His reply to the charge just made is in his fourth stanza, which allows him the chance of an extra summary statement in his fifth stanza. "Yes, I like it here," he says in a reply reminiscent of Yeats's "I am content to live it all again / And yet again. . ." in "A Dialogue of Self and Soul," "Make it twenty times worse / and I'd still do it over again, even with you / like a monkey on my back." Body has accused Soul of being "a scratcher of scabs that are not / there," "An ectoplasmic jitter," and offers the difficulties he has borne, such as the physical punishments Body bore for the sake of the Soul's finicky sense of perfection, reading, writing, and revising. Body charges Soul with being "a glowworm. A spook. A half-strung zither / with a warped sounding box" incapable of true music, in fact comparable to "an alley cat / in moon-heat on a trashcan. . . ." But Soul had evidently nurtured the poet along, and so is now a "dried-out wet-nurse," under delusion that it is the true poet. As far as poetry is concerned, Body charges Soul with being "wind that blew / on ashes that wouldn't catch." The ultimate repudiation is based on the poet's knowledge of poetry, by which "You were gone / the instant I learned the poem is belly and bone." Body is certain that "death's no breather," and "*yes*, I want it all—grab, gaggle, and rut. . . ." Soul is charged with being dead, presumably with the meaning of dead to active influence on the mature poet, though it is Body that makes the charge. Body comes out as might be expected for "the bright brace / of today's air" and the "glitter" (even if it be that of appearance only) of "time and place." He affirms the corporeal qualities with all of their contingencies. The aesthetic of "belly and bone" is very likely one of the things that came as a result of such a teacher as John Holmes with his remark on student Ciardi's poem, "All right, you're haunted. When does it begin to haunt me?"

One of the best of Ciardi's poems on the subject of his father appears here with the title "My Father Died Imperfect as a Man." The details are basically the same familiar ones. If they are not literally true to actual fact, they are obsessively true to the poet's conception of himself and of life and death. The father "died imperfect as a man," as any man will, but "My mother lied him to perfections." The mother was incapable of anything else; it was instinctual. The boy had to guess the truth, in the midst of bizzare rituals of kneeling every night to the saint his obsessed mother had created. Every supernatural faculty was attributed to the saint. His prying eyes say through the blackness within the child, "imperfect as a boy and growing worse." The boy was fortunate in being able to love the haunted mother who had haunted him as well. From this experience, he "forgave myself and learned how to forgive." "Love," so much an answer in Ciardi's system of values, "must intend realities," he says. Thus, he can "be anything but saintly and still live / my father's love, imperfect as a man." The haunting image of the father, long since realized to be different from his mother's obsessive hagiographic image, in teaching the unintended lesson of imperfection, of love, of forgiveness or mercy, makes a quiet but haunting poem fit to be put with the poet's best efforts on the subject.

"A Sentiment for December 25" gives the most forthright analysis of the human situation in terms of Ciardi's give-and-take ironies to be found anywhere in his work. It is explicit, lacking in subtlety but not in profundity. The tone is solemn as a prayer, which it is in everything but name. The conclusion is equally explicit with the Ciardi "message":

> Let mercy be its name till its name be found.
> And wish that to the mercy that is possible because it takes
> nothing from us and may, therefore, be given indifferently,
> there be joined the mercy that adds us to one another. (58)

If this is inconsiderable as a poem, it is not inconsiderable as a moral position. Other poems in *Person to Person* exemplify these points in more conventionally poetic manners.

"Wholly Numbers or The Meditations of Saint Stitch" is the title of the third group of poems in *Person to Person*. Three titles may represent the poems at their best: the title poem of the section, "Meditations of Saint Stitch," " 'Nothing Is Really Hard but to Be Real—' " which Miller Williams used for the title of his introductory essay to *The Achievement of John Ciardi*, and "The Starry Heavens, the Moral Law."

We are never told the identity of Saint Stitch. In his "Meditations" are speculations on the nature of language and its relation to experience, and therefore on the poet's calling, as well as other ideas that are not new to Ciardi's work. Is Stitch a personification of the old saying about "a stitch in time," or some analogue for the principle of stitching things together that are apart or have been torn asunder—stitch rather than graft, weld, meld or other seamless jointure? (Insofar as the author has taken to instructing the nation, one feels this is involved in his phrase.) Surely, there is a pun in "Wholly Numbers," but what would be the nature of the "holy" in this context other than the benign thoughts of the home-made saint? Even that is easier to solve than "Numbers." Evidently, it means "verses," as it had been used in the seventeenth century by Robert Herrick in "Noble Numbers." In which case, what does "Wholly" mean? Entirely, completely poems? One would hope so. Ernest Sandeen said the pun was on Holy Verses, and suggested "stitch (a line of verse)" as the word play.[15]

The narrator invites the reader to ponder his own reactions to the title of "Nothing Is Really Hard but to Be Real—" which is in the form of a one-sided argument. The narrator's voice is one familiar to Ciardi's readers, close to that of the poet himself. Does this title seem "wisdom," "perception," a "gem" of thought? Then he gives his position: ". . . the line is fraudulent," no more than a "blurb," even though any number of "devoutly intellectual / journals" would buy any number of such lines and if they rhymed right call them a sonnet. He explores the charge that he is a cynic, and on the basis of "one wife, three children, and other invest- / ments" concludes, "I'm something else." The line is "gnomic garbage," such as would be used by the devil disguised as a kindly old ham. Unless "carefully warned," all of us "will accept such noises / as examples of the sound an actual mind makes." To accept as authentic such empty rhetoric is to hear the wrong tone, to think genuine what is spurious. Since the poem is intent to suggest a definition of the true, the genuine, the authentic in the human, we must seek "the truth of our own sound." For the true tone, we must study men present and past, read "more poets than jurists (without scorning / Law)," and when we read listen less for the oration than "for its resemblance to that sound in which / we best hear most of what a man is." Once that sound is in our heads, we are able to exclude the others in judgment, for we will have become true listeners. To such a trained ear, the devil with all his guises and blandishments will be able to put forth "only that sound which is exactly *not* the music." Ciardi, for all that he has denied many of the great traditional idealisms such as Christianity, is an inveterate idealist, let his lively mind undercut the doctrines as it will. Idealism, qualified by the humanistic starting point, becomes not the spiritual truths of a Plato with their objective if ethereal existence or the like, but a conception of man that is ever aware of the possibilities of his becoming better than he is. It may never happen, but even to think of the possibility is to have a life raft in the immense sea of modern uncertainty.

Ciardi is not less aware in the poem "Styles" that "A universe is a lot to miss. / But our not missing it won't be missed." His answer is still, couched in rather highflown terms for this poet, *"Thank you / for the experience which I, lovingly, did not / understand."* Those lines from "The Starry Heavens, the Moral Law" are a summary inscription suggested for a tombstone, but with the added Ciardi touch that the stone be made into a bench: "Anyone / who will stop by another man's life may need to sit down." If Ciardi is as he suggested more of a "saying" than a "singing" poet, this poem is one of his fullest utterances. He begins by converting Kant's two grand sources of awe named in the title to a Law: *"everyone would like Heaven as a second skin."* In his relation to the universe, Man the puny, on the edge of "some fabulous system we sense above and far off," has imagined himself "the size and center, and called it Father and Love." Man in the social aspect of his relation to other men is equally muddled but must come to some terms with the sense we have of a "compact" by which "we are related to one another. . . ." For all of our wanderings from it, our violations that betray ourselves, we still "think to call that, Man." There is no objective truth; there is the speculation, the surmise, the dream of men's minds: "Anything can find its dream / in anything: it is there to be found." No matter what condition or circumstance "we are born to, / a mystery will follow." If condition or circumstance were different, men would adapt to them, whatever they are, and take them into account in their world. Men "do / need one another. The rest we adapt to." No matter what changed circumstances men were in, men would find their "mysteries and imaginings" in them, need them, and each other. For "Separation is the one death. As life is / the fitting and refitting of what we shall never quite / join." Whatever we are, it is "unsayable to ourselves." For himself, then, the narrator will settle for the inscription, already quoted. The essential message of the 157-line "Letter of Virginia Johnson" in *Live Another Day* has been restated and updated in a scant forty-seven lines. The definition of man is approximately the same, as is the position in regard to man and his ultimates. Yet any lover of poetry would prefer the later poem, for it is one of Ciardi's finest affirmations of life in all of its unknowable, unrealizable qualities. It is one of the finest sayings of the saying poet, as the volume *Person to Person* is one of his richest.

V   This Strangest Everything *(1966)*

With the publication of this volume, Ciardi's reputation seems to be at low tide. One is forced to surmise the reason. The book itself does not have as much to do with it as a kind of romantic taste for novelty, for the biggest or the littlest, the worst, the best, and so on, on the part of American readers and reviewers, especially the latter. The book itself is a solid accomplishment, if not one of its author's best. It has his typical qualities in forms and themes. He has acquired no new territory, scaled no new heights, plumbed no new depths. Instead, he has once more quietly cultivated his own garden. In a poet so committed to the here and now and his responses to them, possibly one could say it was a bad time; but one could equally say, with Dickens, that it was the best of times, it was the worst of times. William Stafford put it nicely: "he stands for the ready man caught up but not overwhelmed by his time. . . ."[16]

In his review of *Person to Person*, William Dickey had related Ciardi to what is before him: "The quality that I find most notable in Mr. Ciardi is that of observation: he sees things with an intensity and accuracy that no conventional language can wholly contain. . . . Mr. Ciardi's objects break these bounds [of convention]; his sight is defined by the object itself, he accepts and uses the object's own recalcitrance toward language that will soften it." Here he cites an example to indicate that Ciardi's phrase "is wholly determined by what its object looks like, rather than by a kind of language that is felt to be appropriate to the discussion of objects in general." None of Ciardi's subjective responses ever "prevent[s] him from seeing what is before him. This ability to see is neither easy nor usual, and it represents one of the most important ways in which the floating world of poetic language can be given a persistent human relevance, a persistent reference back to the solidities of existence."[17]

Ciardi himself quotes these lines approvingly. He sees them as evidence that he might have achieved "style" rather than "a style." By the former, he means "the way the medium is used to forward what used to be called 'the subject' and is now generally called 'the aesthetic experience' "; whereas, by the latter, he means "the way the medium is used to forward the author's individuality." He is aware, of course, that no poem can contain one to the entire exclusion of the other, though he suspects that the contemporary taste prefers the merely "signatory" to the "representational (whether of outward appearances or of inner-response-to). . . ." This poet believes the representational is the better of the two, but who else other than Ciardi, a mature writer well along in a succcessful career, would say, "I do not know enough about who I am to settle for 'a style.' " These thoughts lead him to the dream of an accomplishment in "a few poems, each in its own voice, and with no two voices co-signatory, but with each (if only hopefully) formed to the subject-experience rather than to one habituated way of speaking." That is, he wants "an act of language so entirely responsive to the poetic experience that my habituated way of speaking will be shattered and leave only the essential language called into being by the aesthetic experience." He sees the ultimate aspect to be his old dream of speaking for himself yet at the same time speaking for every man, for he wants "the poem . . . to declare not 'X spoke these words in his unique way' but rather 'man spoke these words of himself.' "[18]

The point for the consideration of *This Strangest Everything* is that Ciardi in pursuance of these and related ideas has written a simple book, clearly expressed. If he has not achieved his dream entirely, neither has he betrayed it. These things lead into what may be the most notable feature of *This Strangest Everything*, namely, its vocal qualities, or from the side of the audience, its aural qualities. Though the colloquial quality has been strong in Ciardi's poems from the start, there is if anything a new limpidity to these poems. In this sense, the volume is experimental. We lack a real convention to guide the poet in such an endeavor. The sixteenth-century lyricists wrote poems to be sung that were different in nature from the poems that by the end of the century were written to be read from the printed page. There were a few things in Donne, a few in Wordsworth, others in Browning to be read aloud, but none of these would suffice to aid a twentieth-century poet in writing simply and naturally. Since we have no living tradition of song in modern poetry and no adequate definition of lyric verse, what is a poet to do? There are various rhetorical poems that use the speaking voice, especially in an exalted or extreme manner; also, there are various quiet utterances, especially the musings of neurotic or isolated characters. For these, there is more or less a tradition to measure such efforts by. Ciardi, with his interest in the quotidian, the transient, the minor, the ordinary, the personal, has had to forge his own medium of expression for such things. *This Strangest Everything* is his answer to the problem. His frequent metaphor for individual qualities, which by intention extends to the human in general, is sound, tone, the speaking voice. And what more typifies men than their voices? Any man than his voice? Without eschewing any of his other qualities, Ciardi has here written a volume that goes best when read aloud, when heard. The poems are easy to say, are clever and witty, employ their author's frequent themes, but certain difficulties that appeared in other poems are contained and limited by what the speaking voice can say, naturally. There is little here that could not be said in actual conversation, though the dross of most of our conversations is absent. In token of these qualities, Ciardi has read most of the poems on two Spoken Arts Recordings. The ideal of writing for the speaking voice, for his own unique voice, had long been a principle with Ciardi, though never achieved as fully as in *This Strangest Everything*. In poems profounder than they may seem, the saying poet here truly has his say.

The result for his reputation, however, was that, by and large, he was ignored or chided by reviewers for his lack of discrimination in regard to his work. Ciardi appears in his full maturity to be a poet to please the audience more than the critics. This is not uncommon with living poets whose careers are long. Of the two, Ciardi would probably prefer the readers, just as he had once spoken up for the person of some general culture. With the critics, he deserves better, more tolerance and more apt comparisons.

The first group of seventeen poems in *This Strangest Everything* is called "The Longest Way Is Back." In several notable poems, the poet looks at life from the point of view of aging, well-fed affluence. "Talking Myself to Sleep at One More Hilton" strikes this note as well as any. It was later used as one of the frame poems for *Lives of X*. The plight of the narrator is that much-commented-on one typical of Americans in which the objects that marked and shaped their experiences have gone under the wrecking ball and the bulldozer, nominally to make way for the new signs and bearings of a juggernaut progress:

> I have a country but no town.
> Home ran away from me. My trees
> ripped up their white roots and lay down.
> Bulldozers cut my lawn.[19]

He runs over the remembered details of that vanished house and childhood, which included trees to climb, "behave and misbehave," "lamb stew,'" "sin," "house," "chicken run," "garden," "guilt," "rocking chair," "six dogs and every one / was killed in traffic." The graves, once known, are now forgotten. An overpass came which altered the quality of the life possible in the house. The things of sentiment have perished in fact. The interesting point is the narrator's response, most interesting in its hesitance: "I wonder if I really mind." The dogs and all lie buried "where time was / when time still flowed, where now a slate / stiff river loops, called Exit Nine." For the losses that were once all of reality, compensations have come, again put with a certain hesitancy: "I have the way I think I live." There are the expense accounts, jet planes that mount the clouds, and good bourbon, for "My father's house is Hilton-wide." These are put against the old dog bones and the still speculative "Were my trees / still standing would I really care?" Is it not a disease with a name to wish that everything would remain unchanged if one were to revisit, which one "will not / and never meant to"? After what was almost a moment of weakness and regret comes the positive aspect: "I am not and mean not to be / what I was once." The dimensions in the present affluence are vaster, coast to coast, bridgeable in five hours, "soon to be three." The terms give this away as less than fully, humanly satisfying: ". . . home is anywhere between." The new certainties—are they not those of affluent America as well?—are airport limousines, credit, the inevitable drink, "the best steak you ever had." And in the midst of the deracinated rush there is always "thinking—when there's time to think—" As to the entire life,

> it's good enough. At least not bad.
> Better than dog bones and lamb stew.
> It does. Or it will have to do. (8)

There is a very nice doubleness and a tone to match in this poem. Any mature American will have to admit the necessity for the enumerated items to fall out of existence save to the sentimental memory. As Ciardi poses them, they are not of great value among the things that ought to survive. Yet it is the Ciardi touch and part of the excellence of the poem that the terms of experience that have replaced them are not made attractive in their presentation. In fact, they seem even more fleeting. When put with the title, one gets the sense of a muddled modern, uncertain equally about the past and the present, who is fighting down doubts that are never quite uttered about the worth of modern American life. And yet, how can one not live it, to a large degree? The note of suppressed urgency or desperation, contained with effort, ending with a small bit of consolatory wisdom on the positive side just barely, uncertain still, yet resigned—these add up to a fine poem in the colloquial ease of Ciardi's mature manner which has the ability to hold in tension the multiple contradictions that are unavoidable in modern life. The poem is similar to several others by Ciardi, yet no two are quite alike. In casting over the circumstances of prosperous American life, searching for significance, for meaning, for what we should do now, he is a long way in external details from the big Italian boy hoping desperately to win some of the Hopwood money nearly thirty years before, but his flight is still "homeward to America."

The second section, comprising sixteen poems, is entitled "A Black-Bread Store." It is about creativity, in the artist and in the world of nature, if a common theme can be found. The one is no more to be put to narrow human purposes than the other. The purpose of each is to fulfill its own ends, and the first is to embody its own kind of life. Readers of *How Does a Poem Mean?* will recognize this idea as a version of Ciardi's many-times-repeated statement that the function of a poem is to perform itself, though performance and self cannot be separated except for convenience of discussion.

The title comes from a metaphor in "Why Don't You Write for Me?" which begins with the poet in full confidence enlightening the possible reader who asked the question. The poet replies, "For you, or of you? It can't be / both. If you must ask that / question, you are not ready for / yourself." The reason is the correspondence between a living self and a poem. To conceive something entirely, as a self, is to move beyond it in the living continuum that does not end in this life. But on the basis of what men have in common, poems are possible in which communication can take place, if not for everyone—impossible ideal!—then for the few:

> If I write for
> you, I must write about someone
> else: someone dead, though you
> haven't heard of that death. If of
> you, you haven't heard that
> news either. Then what can I tell you? (41)

The logic is sophistical, of course, but makes sense in that world of irony and paradox that poets tell us of, in which, as so many poets have phrased it, a poet lies in order to tell the truth. But in this case, the poem is immediately an answer to the asker of the question of the title. Ciardi proceeds with a metaphor of poetry as a business, just as Yeats with a variety of ironic intentions often called the writing of poetry a "trade." The business metaphor is developed throughout the rest of the poem. If the customers are few, there is no matter, because the poet lives "by eating up the profits." Examine it anyway you like, "there is always a profit, / and it can always be eaten. . . ." This is not in any sense to scorn the "customers" who are welcome, even cherished. The next development is interesting for what it implies about the author's conception of poetry. He stocks nothing he cannot "live by / when no customers come." Thus, the customer's taste must approach the proprietor's if commerce is to take place. Limited this may be, but far from entire loss:

> A black-bread
> store, if you like. Stiff crusts and
> garlicky cores. But learn to like it
> and nothing can feed you better. (42)

Obviously, the poet's product is not a purely commercial one. This poem would appear to suggest that the poet cannot reach all men no matter what he does, though conceivably he still can speak of and for them, at the same time writing of and for himself. Let his confection reach those it can.

This is conceivably Ciardi's response to a declining critical favor, while his mastery of his chosen idiom is finer than ever. Every artist has to write some such poem in his career: if he has had an early audience, he outstrips it, to the clamorous cries for a return to what no longer concerns him; if he is late in acquiring an audience, he dreams of the connection being made at last, perhaps idealizing it somewhat. This theme is not impossibly far from the faith in art as something to outlive frail human beauty, such as the Elizabethan sonneteers used, drawing on an old tradition. Ciardi's version is just a little bleaker, being modern, in that it poses the possibility of no "customers," no recognition. It shares more in spirit with Kafka's "A Hunger Artist," in which the artist at starving surpassed himself in neglect, out of the sight of an audience which, fickle, had taken up the craze of black panthers and would not believe the feat of the artist anyway. However easy the manner of Ciardi's poem, the commitment is real. His whole approach to life as making do with what one has is brought home to his own art, with all attendant ironies.

The third section of *This Strangest Everything*, "Pencil Stub Journals," contains fourteen poems, one of them, with the same title, containing twenty-three short poems in the manner of epigrams. The entire section was singled out by one commentator, as close to "the sloppy, the witless, the totally unprofitable."[20] Another singled out the group of twenty-three as "worthy of the few masters of the kind."[21] Actually, they are more than the former and less than the latter. One of the best is "On Leaving the Party After Having Been Possibly Brilliant for Certainly Too Long," though it is as much like a regular Ciardi poem as like an epigram. The narrator is "smiled out, talked out, quipped out, socialized . . ." out of his own identity, and needs "mortal silences" to come back to the self he must live with daily.

Ciardi has cleverness, a good mind for irony and paradox, and a good perception for what William Stafford called "slant moral issues."[22] These qualities, which he had from his earliest published work, stand him in good stead when it comes to epigrams, but one feels that, like the imagist poem he writes occasionally, the epigram does not engage him except in passing.

From *This Strangest Everything* as a whole, one comes away with the distinct impression that the typical Ciardi position is here, and it is basically positive, even when it seems negative. In a secular way, he manages to affirm life and human experience despite every contingency, almost, but not quite, *because* of the contingencies. Life is its own end and justification, its own chief danger to itself; though man's mind cannot solve the human puzzle, it must and will keep trying. Any reader of American literature will see the similarity between Ciardi's work and the ironic affirmation of our major writers from Hawthorne to the present. Ciardi's saying voice speaks an authentic American dialect.

CHAPTER 4

Remembrance of Things Past—and Back Again

I   Lives of X *(1971)*

IN *Lives of X* (1971), Ciardi has written the closest thing to a formal autobiography he has yet attempted. The basic story is the familiar one he has told all his writing life. New details are added only. Structurally, the book comprises two frame poems from earlier volumes; in between is a meditation on fortune as it has pertained to his own life, followed by twelve selected episodes arranged chronologically from the poet's infancy to his maturity. They are in the modern manner as it has been achieved in both poetry and prose and make full use of allusion, juxtaposition, ellipsis, synecdoche, nonsequential narration, and symbolism; the whole is cast in Ciardi's flexible colloquial idiom. A more detailed analysis is forthcoming. Yet the very title suggests many things about his conception of himself. Both substantive terms of the title are significant—"lives" and "X." The second is the American means to indicate anonymity and thus the typical or representative. In this author's case, by his own account in several places, it means undefined in any final way, still unfinished. With this vital and creative personality, only death will do such finishing, one feels. A possibility of extra meaning would be to regard X as the Greek *chi*, symbol for cross, Christ, and Christianity; however, the poems themselves, despite the religious references from the author's Catholic childhood in an Italian immigrant family, nullify this possibility, which would include a kind of martyrdom in America, land of opportunity.

The other term, "lives," suggests the discrete nature of the experiences related and the intensity. To a reader the pieces of life can easily seem to fall into a typically American kind of unity, that of the American success story in which an unlikely origin in a humble and obscure family becomes less handicap than impetus to the American dream of success. Benjamin Franklin set the pattern for this response, but this later episode from the American mythology includes things Ben did not anticipate, such as the Great Depression, both close enough to present-day Americans to be real and far enough into the past to be reality that has itself become legend. Such a reading is not untrue, but it would miss the intensity of the experiences of *Lives of X*. In a sense, this should have been Ciardi's first book, had he been able to write it. When he goes back over the materials of his early life, he recaptures some of the passionate intensity of his earlier poetry that had gradually become, in the later, irony and acceptance, even wisdom. Besides, Franklin wrote in the context of certainties which few modern writers can share. Any honest modern foray into the past is bound to be exploratory, seeking for values and meanings, and the intrepid explorer is as likely as not to return empty-handed. Some such perspective on Ciardi's work resulted in the most penetrating evaluation it has received in years, John Hughes's "Humanism and the Orphic Voice," which appeared in the poet's own journal, *Saturday Review* (May 22, 1971, pp. 31–33).

If critical esteem exists in any correlation to the number of reviews a book receives, then Ciardi's reputation was at its lowest ebb, a fact he modestly noted in a 1973 interview. In answer to the question, "Do you feel your work is being understood by the people you want to understand it?" Ciardi replied:

Can anyone say that? It's hard to give an honest answer to that, especially since I have a feeling that in many ways I've been one of the most rewarded poets in American literature: the lecture circuit, people are always asking me to talk, my books sell. Yet, odd as it may seem, I think I had three reviews across the country of my last book of poems (*Lives of X*). I thought it was something of a technical breakthrough. I can't help thinking it deserved a little more critical comment than that. I think I have added a dimension to what's available simply because contemporary poets have given away fictional technique to the short story writers. And in *Lives of X* I think I've returned a lot of fictional technique to poetry in what I feel works. I think that might have been worth a comment.[1]

Miller Williams, to whom the book is dedicated, had remarked in passing the connection with the short story and surmised that his friend might be the starting point for a new or revived trend toward narrative in contemporary poetry. If the phenomenon has not come about in any noticeable way, the failed prediction in no way alters the quality of Ciardi's book of "stories."

The poet's interest may understandably be in his new technical acquisitions, but a reader takes those things for granted unless they fail. Despite critical neglect, Ciardi's *Lives of X* did not fail. He had been the master of narrative every time he tried it in the past, though usually the stories concentrated on a few of the elements found in the short story. The stories in *Lives of X* try for them all. The earlier ones had usually centered on one character and one situation. Setting was incidental. Attitude and tone followed appropriately. Theme was more or less circumscribed by the other limitations, but occasionally forced onto the materials by the author. In the new poems, setting in place and time and circumstances is expanded, quite in keeping with the theme of the American experience. Characterization is given detailed and careful attention so that a whole gallery of characters comes to life out of an American past otherwise lost to general awareness. Unlike those in many autobiographies, these come to life in their own right, apart from their relations to the narrator. The real pulse of the book and the subject that has never failed him is his loving depiction of his Italian family and connections, its experiences, and its various meanings. Occasionally Ciardi will pay back an old score, as in "Cal Coolidge and the Co" against head clerk Judson Treadlowe Marshall, who had hired the boy to work in 1933 but circumspectly required a kickback in the form of a new Stetson hat which took most of the first week's salary. The Boston Irish, especially the priests, are treated scathingly. Rhythm, very much the essence of poetry in Ciardi's view, is a technical problem he solved, according to Robert Wallace, by "a comfortable blank verse not far from prose" and in a style "occasionally prosy, discursive. . . ."[2] To the present writer's sense, these things are more seeming than actual. In the best tradition of both the short story and the short poem, Ciardi has managed to be as loose and slow-paced as needed but also when needed compact and concentrated. He has his own way with diction and syntax by which he controls the pace of the poem's movement. Lines seemingly loose and casual can suddenly have clusters of density and back again. Diction, syntax, and figurative language are all used with skill. In "Epilogue: The

Burial of the Last Elder" are lines as prosy as "He'd never left but only stretched a visit / into a way of life on a tourist visa / that never quite expired . . ." alternating with "He was the last where none / could sing the yokel cadence of his mountain— / not dialect but defeat, a tribe's long waste / from father stones it could no longer read. . . ." Once again, the aspect of the poems Ciardi himself singled out for attention from the neglect of his few commentators is new only in the broader scope of his ambition. And his grasp is at the least adequate for his reach when it is not better than that.

If most critics ignored not just the narrative accomplishments but the entire book, the one who did not gave it the kind of searching analysis any poet ought to desire. John W. Hughes, "free-lance writer and critic," gave *Lives of X* the major attention in a review that discussed other books as well (by Hugh MacDiarmid, James Wright, and Beth Bentley, and even a book on Robinson Jeffers). Ciardi's books in the past had been reviewed mostly by librarians who were obliged to say what audience the books should suit, or else by fellow poets who, understandably, noticed his technical accomplishment and singled out passages that handled a theme in excellent fashion. Hughes, evidently neither of these, is more concerned with the nature of the vision of existence and its truth. He has an electic vision with a set of values of his own that seems put together from Elizabeth Sewell's *The Orphic Voice* (1960) and from several existentialist philosophers. The "Orphic voice" results from "the poetic vision of a unity that is unknown to 'cool reason.' " Hughes takes a passage from "The River," a poem which should be put against the earlier "Mystic River," and makes something almost mystical out of it:

> It was my country and a mystery sung
> by bird, by brook, by squirrels chattering,
> and shadows through the trees and old lies told
> and histories tipping truths. (23)

To Hughes, this "mystery" becomes "the Orphic interconnection of existence, the vast language of the cosmos that is given supreme expression in the microcosm of the poem." Further, this "orphic voice is subversive in that it breaks down the subject-object distinctions of the Cartesian mind. . . ." This is not to deny a duality between subject and object, for "the poem is founded

upon the I-Thou relation established between poet and world,"
but "Ciardi shows that such a relation is 'ahead of thought' "
(Ciardi's phrase). Hughes adds that "it is the ground of human
feeling upon which a healthy rationality can be erected." In their
generality, these remarks would fit Wordsworth as easily as Ciardi, though in illustration the English poet would be committed
to Hartleyan empiricism and the American would not. Hughes
invokes Wordsworth by name and might have made further use
of him, for *Lives of X* is Ciardi's *Prelude.* Like the English poet,
Ciardi does ponder subject-object relationships, family, schooling
both formal and personal, and so on. If Wordsworth had seen his
beloved English rivers and lakes poisoned the way Ciardi's Mystic
River was, the *Prelude* might have been about the growth of a
different kind of mind. Hughes gives Ciardi credit, along with
Robert Lowell, Stanley Kunitz, and others, for regaining for
poetry "the Romantic sense of existential subjectivity" that Eliot
and Pound swathed in aesthetic theories. Rather than being a
frozen Imagistic instant, time in *Lives of X* is "a vehicle for the existential encounter between poet and world." In working out the
details of the social context of his poems, Ciardi "establishes a
profound dialectic between Id and Ego, lunacy and Orphic
order." He "refuses to glorify (or simplify) insanity and regres-
sion. . . ." Since Hughes on this point plays Ciardi off against
"such trendy Poundian irrationalists as Michael McClure and
Gregory Corso," *his* values become apparent, and apparently
similar to those of his subject. If Hughes sees man doomed to the
choices of the existential moment, still reason and civilization are
possible in some fashion, and most immediately, so is art. Hughes
makes one other point worth noting, about "The Graph," a poem
he regards as "probably his most successful poem to date," but it
would not be wrong to say the same thing of the best of this poet's
work in general. The graph "that totals up the number of enemy
dead" is the central symbol of the poem, and it "is at all points inseparable from the poet's experience; it is never imposed *on* that
experience. . . ." In Hughes's view, this is a real achievement.

Ciardi's humansim has been remarked too many times in this
study to need reiterating at this point. One point must be made,
however. Hughes has shown several possibilities for responses to
Ciardi's work that no one else has attempted. However, the
qualities he notes do not appear for the first time in *Lives of X* but
in their degree are pervasive throughout Ciardi's work. Miller

Williams has covered most of them in different terms, and the present writer has noted them in still different ones. Many are the qualities of poetry itself, especially from Wordsworth on. The point is that the terms Hughes uses are not necessary ones for an appreciation of Ciardi, but others will serve as well. This is said with no intention to undercut a brilliant essay on a book worth far more attention than it ever got.

The book itself contains fifteen poems. The first is "The Evil Eye" from *From Time to Time* and the last is "Talking Myself to Sleep at One More Hilton" from *This Strangest Everything*. As Ciardi described it, "These poems are not properly part of the present sequence but are meant to serve something like the function of a frame around a canvas. It was Miller Williams who suggested I use them in this way and his suggestion, as usual, made sense."[3] The suggestion is a brilliant one, especially if the book is regarded as an entity separate from the author's other work. The latter has been noticed earlier in the present study. "The Evil Eye" gives an account of the birth of the future poet in the Italian peasant context, surrounded by a midwife and other immemorial old women working spells to insure the babe's future and to read it. A nun prays and offers "a scapular stitched with virgin's hair" in an effort to ward off the evil eye one crone has perceived. The babe received his first name at baptism before he was ready for either the forecasted evil or his own name, though, as he later said, "I had one already and the other came." The book is, of course, an account of the name he attained and what the life was (or lives were) that sustained it. The frame poem at the other end is, in this context, a kind of triumphant if ironic commentary on the theme of the name. The well-to-do, sought-after man with the expense account finds his name honored nationwide; ironically, it is only for the money it will bring. The bearer values the money, of course, but not supremely. The name means many other things to him. So, the frame poems have the important function of tightening up the narratives in between. They are not necessary but, like the right picture frame, set off the qualities of what they frame.

The poem "Prologue: Letter to an Indolent Norn" sets forth the best overall interpretation of the material, in which young Ciardi is a veritable "Lucky John," despite every limitation, every travail, every obstacle. The land of opportunity was just that for him, despite the lifelong coruscations of his irony on that land, its

history, its life and times. The Norn is in effect the circumstances
and facts of his life. The poem is one more résumé of that life and
a stocktaking of its inventory. Ciardi goes very much against the
prevailing temper of modern times in that he is reconciled to his
past. He gives thanks for his parents, "Because they were crude
and easy and without fixed expectation / and could, therefore,
accept what they got from me . . ." from whom he "left with no
baggage but love." The father killed, the mother "maddened" by
her fate ended as a "witless" old woman crying about practically
everything, including eventually the fear that the cost of her
upkeep would turn the son from her. Through nearly every item
of his inventory, Ciardi ponders the pattern. Was it intended, or
was it accidental? For example, his youthful religious ecstasy and
agony eventually had the effect of simply leaving him bored by
his own zeal. Whatever the pattern is of missed or neglected
chances on the part of his Indolent Norn, he returns thanks, convinced that the reason, if any, is "not to be taken for kindness."
He wishes that all gods might "come to keep such slovenly ways."
The poet is led to brood on the significance:

> Is mercy no more than the fed hawk's drowse?
>   But I have been where you fed. I have felt wings,
>   though never talons. What mercy
>   is made of oversights? I was brushed and ignored. (6)

He ponders his own luck in evading calamity, including World
War II, against examples of those who fared otherwise. Again,
"thank you, for good enough in a bad market. / I have suffered
nothing I could not bear, / pity and not be made to bear." He
was essentially an observer to things others were addicted to, such
as gambling. Being Ciardi, he has to ask, "Is an observer / a good
enough thing?" Is it all a plan "to nag me easy / till I claw myself
in the guilt of not hurting?" He is no more responsible for his own
nature than are the addicts. Various appeals are made to his sense
of pity; he can bear them and turn his response to the small advantage of a tax deduction. Though he himself is "not
indifferent," the Norn's "is the one mercy by indifference.
Mine / is given and taken. I expected less than I have come
to / and can give more than I meant." Presumably, he recalls the
birth experience of "The Evil Eye" and after that his World War
II days when he says he has "died once, knew I would die,

knew / it would make no difference. . . ." Surviving, he gained "Lazarus rights" in which the experience of life had zest and intensity, near to a condition "where being itself / is joy itself. . . ." It was not just luck, for luck is "an innocence." He was either guiltless and therefore allowed to go free, or if guilty has met the terms imposed upon him. His last wish is that the Norn not be stirred from her drowse: "In your whim is our peace. May nothing prompt it / from any indolence that will do for mercy." If the poem is fanciful, that very fancy puts it at sufficient distance from author and reader so that a serious pondering of the nature of destiny may take place. If it is lighthearted, how else should a fortunate man write?

A reader of the Ciardi corpus knows his considerable accomplishment. Nevertheless, one suspects he will not hear an angelic voice such as Rilke thought he heard at Duino Castle; will never undergo anything like the self-transcendence that Pound gained in the *Pisan Cantos* from his incarceration. One is confident the Norn will remain indolent, her charge's accomplishment good but not quite great, any new poems essentially repeating though not outdoing earlier ones. Everything might have been different if . . . but the right form of that utterance is the interrogative, and no mere declarative is sufficient.

The familiar Ciardi materials appear in "The Shaft," and include birth in a tenement in North Boston into a close-knit Italian immigrant family, the father's death, the mother's obsession with the late husband, her lack of comprehension of the strange, non-Italian country to which she had come as a young woman with the high hopes mentioned in the first poem of Ciardi's first book, her troubles aggravated by her difficulties with the language of the place she was never fully a part of. There are many new touches to the portrait of this mother, who was a haunting presence in the poet's life and is a recurrent figure or just referent in his poems. No doubt she was a lifelong trial to her son, with her Old World peasant immensity that was incompatible with modern America; her operatic frenzy appears several times in the poems. Whatever the truth of fact, she is a fascinating character every time she appears in her son's work. In "Three Views of a Mother" (*As If*) she was respectively the grandmother trilling a language from close to nature and known only to grandmothers, children, and perhaps animals; the avid gardener to whom winter is an abomination; the old woman who gathers thirty pounds of mushrooms from the woods (in recording, Ciardi reads it as sixty) and brings them home for praise to her city-bred son, who bears her demands patiently. If the poem is not profound, it has the elemental strength that is present in most of his Italian poems; it is warm and affectionate and done with no wasted touches, though, in this case, the poet's response to the subject is of far less importance than the subject itself.

The same elemental quality comes out in "Daemons," from *This Strangest Everything*. She represents "the demon in things." The other "savages on the street" her son passes "have forgotten how the soul breathes / from plant, beast, and man and must / be propitiated." Their superstitions are shabby, relatively empty; they are "ritualists without conviction." When the son built a new house, the old woman muttered charms over the foundation forms and added items of various kinds, including a drop of blood. As the son puts it in admiration, "She was using everything she knew anything / about, and she knew she was using it." Her value as example is that she was living *at* what she lived *by*, and her importance for the man and poet is that she was the "savage" he learned from. Presumably, in striving the fullest she was capable of, she achieved even more by the effect beyond her comprehension she had on her son. Though the point is not made as such, one of the widening ripples of this pool is surely the poet's faith in his work, the consequences of which he can intend but still not foresee, much less control.

In "Epithalamium at St. Michael's Cemetery," also from *This Strangest Everything*, the woman, "her wits shed / some years before her light," is laid to rest beside her husband, fifty years after his death. The reunion of "the sodden groom, the driftwood bride" is macabre enough to make a casual reader miss the profoundly pessimistic aspect of the poem. It is meditative rather than philosophical, less about the dead mother than about the nature of death in relation to her faith in reunion at last with her young husband. The personal response of the poet is indicated by "Can I find a tear / for what this is? I have none left." The important point to notice here is that wherever a successful poem by Ciardi begins, quite often in personal experience, it stops after involvements and complications have been seen and posed that include our profundities as well as the speaker's, though we have seen them much less clearly and posed them less honestly. If we cannot always resolve them, neither can the author, but that in no way nullifies the poem or lessens the value of Ciardi's work.

If the mother was merely the beginning point of a meditation on nothingness in the "Epithalamium," she is a living and vital individual in *Lives of X*, notably "The Shaft" and "A Five-Year Step." She is an important presence or reference in other of the poems. Evidently, in her grief and fear in the alien land and tongue where even god's vicars spoke the language she comprehended little, she made the dead husband into a kind of saint to whom she talked and prayed. She woke from nightmares, near to hysteria. The son had to learn how much of this was a style of acting, how much real, and "how much more / could be the actress acting what she was. . . ." Part of their purpose, as he eventually saw, was to draw the remains of the family close around her. While the daughters ministered to the mother, the son "lay / guilty of happiness, half deep in books. . . ." Suspicious of the girls' evening strolls, she crept spying after them, only to be led on lengthy and circuitous routes designed to tease her. When she realized their pranks, she resorted to fainting spells and would not be revived until all her fledglings hovered in an anxious guilty circle about her, as in grand opera. The son, looking back, can say, "I didn't know she was crazy. That we all were." Eventually, all of the children realized the faints were put on for the occasion. In desperation, the son, "an actor, too, /from a family of actors," guessed that his "best chance was to play her husband." His jocularity that was "Just like your father, pig!" was only partially successful. From smile to giggle to mad laughter to scream that was not put on, she moved, out of a well of fear too deep for the boy to be "husband to," but his later observation is that all madness is fear. She recovered partially, and "did ease into age with half a smile / mending inside her," but went into a muttering senility in her eighties in which she recognized nothing outside her own subjectivity. The native-born son was much better able to cope with the new world that was part of her fear, but by his own accounts she taxed him exceedingly. Many a failed person would grab the boon of such a mother and such a family situation as self-evident cause of his failures. Not Ciardi. Instead, he grew in moral stature, from unavoidable acceptance to understanding to forgiveness, compassion, and to love despite all, which, in the long run, is the only kind. It is the active ingredient in his much-used term "mercy."

Coming to terms at home with his difficult mother was part of

Ciardi's definition of self. A later definition, in "A Five-Year
Step," meant both literally and symbolically, was that

> we were Greeks who spoke ourselves in bad Italian
> from a parish of goat thickets, civil war,
> and hot blood on the mountain—all our saints
> disguised as Catholic but as mountain-rank
> as a day's sweat on the ledges of the starved
> who put their prayers into thickets. (72)

(And in a "Manner of Speaking" piece, he demonstrated ety-
mologically that his name came from the Lombards and was
ultimately German.) In between the two definitions came important growth in which the mother figured. A petty Irish priest was
conducting a kind of impromptu catechism with the children of
his predominantly Irish parishioners. "Where did St. Patrick
come from?" and "Where did he bring his blessing?" he asked to
screamed answers of "Ireland! Ireland!" The third question got a
different answer. "And where did your fathers come from?"
Young Ciardi in a supreme assertion of identity heard his own
voice bellowing, "FROM ITALY, BY GOD!" When the priest
dragged him by one ear to the altar with the angry instructions to
"PRAY FOR YOUR SOUL!" he fled, prepared to be damned
before denying himself. He knew he had a whipping to undergo
from his mother whenever he returned home. Her ceremonial in-
strument of punishment, used for extreme cases, was a homemade
"cat-of-twenty tails" made of rolled leather cut into strips. He
withstood the brutal punishment without a whimper, whereupon
the mother broke into tears. He threw the cat into the garbage,
mother and son kissed, "And both of us knew it was my confirma-
tion." Melodramatic it was, but he had frightened her and taken
a mutually acknowledged step toward manhood. Though the act
was half a fraud on his part, it was important nevertheless. The
boy realized, as his mother tended his wounds, that she saw him
against a scale of values in which the peasant hero of the *lex
talionis* took its pleasure on the wicked *carabinieri*. The lesson he
learned "broke my own madness." He was able to value "the
purity of her madness, which was love / in its own numbered
cave." It was five years later that the now young man had his
manhood and peasant Italian identity solidified in an experience
which involved the mother. The same priest earlier offended

came to talk to the future poet about the state of his soul because he was reading William James's *The Varieties of Religious Experience.* "Heesa no home-a," the young man heard her lie, knowing she knew otherwise, and in response to a lecture on her own possible damnation, "You leava my Johnny alone-a, you Irisha, you. / Heesa goo' boy!" Even at the time, he saw it as a loyalty beyond which there is no other. The "abdicated matriarch," become her son's "daughter," had given him a lesson in immemorial humanness that was "indivisibly ahead of thought." She had given him the lesson of first loyalties and love. He knew on the spot that "I am no man till I am your son." Though the poet may have refined and made these values more subtle, his work shows abundantly that he has never strayed from nor ever betrayed them.

The first poem in his next book, *The Little That Is All,* is "Addio," a last farewell to the dead mother. It manifests sentiment which the reader can accept and participate in. It is not sentimental. Feeling is constrained in a straightforward but tight twelve lines. At her deathbed, the poet saw her change from still-panting corpse to actual death, as though heeding a divine call that said, "Oh, stop that!" Kissing her forehead in its final cold, he thought, "Oh, daughter, if *I* could call!" It is a touching tribute to the mother and son, the father and daughter who were bound "indivisibly ahead of thought," The volume is dedicated to "Concetta DeBenedictis Ciardi in loving memory."

Returning to *Lives of X,* we find in "The River" the family moved to nearby Medford, where the boy passed through an idyllic childhood on the Mystic River; he played where history had been made—and money—by the Puritans with their molasses, rum, and slave trade. Irish Catholics, Italians, and Armenians eventually acquired the land and inherited the tradition which fitted them poorly. The vices of the Puritans more than anything else register with the poet, though as a child he played in their heroic shadow. The changes in the river roughly parallel the changes in the history, as though the sins of the fathers were worked out in the future to the detriment of the landscape as well as the later immigrant arrivals. Despite the tears, suspicions, and obsessions of the mother, the boy ". . . was young and happier than her tears / could change me from."

The education of the boy was an education in disillusionment, as comes out in "A Knothole in Spent Time." Here dressed in in-

appropriate finery by the mother, who was ignorant but respectful of schooling, the boy was told by "a pugnosed Irish snot" that
he "was not only a Dago but a sissy." On his first day in the first
grade of school, when he "had set out to worship and be saved,"
he had to fight, which with its ripped buttons and grass stains and
dried blood about the nose also meant a strapping from the
mother. The child was tough enough for that. Another experience
was more shattering and long-lived. The teacher, designated as
Miss Matron-Column but a symbol of Omniscience to the innocent Italians, mispronounced his name as "John Sea-YARD-i":

> I had been rechristened. All the way through high school
> and my little while at Bates and my time at Tufts
> —at both of which there were kids I'd started school with—
> I was Sea-YARD-i. It took me seventeen years
> and a bus ride out to Michigan—out past Canada—
> to make my escape. And the first thing I did, free,
> was to get rid forever of Matron-Column's
> last ghost upon me and get my own ghost back
> the way it sounded when its ghost began. (29–30)

One more great acquisition came in these early school days. He
progressed from Miss Matron-Column to Miss Absolute Void,
who became

> . . . the first chink in the wall
> of heavens I had been schooled to as a faith,
> though she didn't know it, and couldn't have been told.
> I doubt she could have guessed the wall was there. (32)

Called upon to read, the daydreaming boy had recited from
memory the lesson and only pretended to read. The great revelation was that he had fooled a teacher, but who would believe
him?

> I was alone
> my first time into the world, at an edge of light
> that dizzied like a dark; my gloat, half fear,
> my eye at its first peephole into heavens
> where Teachers were only people and could be wrong,
> and all Ma's stations and candles could be rounded
> by a truth I'd caught and held, and couldn't tell! (33)

The lesson was profound. As he later told Merrill Moore (in the latter's capacity as friend rather than his professional one of psychiatrist), he had

> . . . found my hole in heaven
> and seen Miss Absolute Void take off her wings
> and soak her feet in a bucket of steaming water,
> and never found a heaven whole again
> nor anyone to tell about what I'd found. (34)

Except the whole world through his poetry, one must add. The strain of pessimism, the theme of human limitations and inadequacies, that so permeates Ciardi's work may have received its initial impetus in a grammar school in Medford, Massachusetts, just as the life-affirming insistence may have begun in the Italian family in which love and exuberance redeemed all of the limitations and handicaps. *Lives of X* makes best sense when put with the author's other books rather than regarded in isolation.

Humor is mixed with compassion and understanding in "Feasts." His Uncle Alec had a friend, Dominic Cataldo, who worked as a treetop trimmer at the rich Forest Hills cemetery and who was the leader of "the last organized gang of pheasant poachers / to operate within the city limits / of Boston, Mass. . . ." Young Ciardi was taken along on furtive Sunday-morning excursions as the "bird dog" for the gang. Cataldo "a long-armed, bow-legged, broken toothed gorilla" with an exceedingly hairy chest, was a master of Sputasangue, literally "Spitblood," an Italian invective in which this "artist" could "stretch a roaring curse / a full ten minutes and not run out of figures / nor use the same one twice." In his mastery, he

> . . . could start
> at the triune top and work the hagiography
> down to St. Fish be strict anatomizings,
> to frottery, battery, buggery, rape, plain mayhem,
> and on to atrocious-assault-with-intent, compounded
> twelve generations back and twenty forward. (37)

Despite herself, even the boy's mother admired "the rhapsode at the root of man, / his flowering tongues." The hungry poachers never had a bag less than sixteen. The gang of three adults (two of

whom were bachelors) and the boy took the birds back to the
Ciardi house where the boy's mother and Aunt Cristina, who had
collected dandelions and mushrooms, dressed and cooked the
catch, whereupon the entire group gorged themselves, slept, and
gorged again. Just as the hunters felt they "harvested God's
hand / and lived well out of it," so to the family "Those birds
were free grace and our week-long meat." Ciardi describes the
other means the desperately poor resorted to for food, gardening
as well as all forms of poaching in season and out, for "a robin in
spaghetti sauce was a meat ball / that didn't have to be bought.
. . ." In keeping with the peasant naiveté, the poem uses religious
imagery frequently—"food and faith and holiday," "a next day's
gift of grace / from open-handed heaven," "God's great day / of
squirrels, rabbits, and anything with wings" and so on. In keeping with the theme of time on which all of the narratives are
strung, the poet jumps to his present state of affluence, which
makes it possible to buy whatever food he wishes. Alec at ninety-
four is toothless and suffers from bad legs but declined his
nephew's offer of first-floor rent, preferring his three-story climb
up stairs. The poem ends with the rueful wish that if the poet had
God's powers, he would send the old man back to those Edenic
Sundays in which he would be again

> My man of plenty, ritual to his friends,
> and honored home and hale, safe in the garden
> that flowered forever, till it wasn't there. (42)

This poem is not even necessarily one of the best in the book, but
it teems with the quality every good autobiography has, not the
life of the narrator which if set forth analytically is likely to be
dull, but of the whole human mystery and color of the human life
in which he was nurtured and took the impress of his own
humanity. Wordsworth might have found a moral in these annals
of the poor, but Ciardi found life and color and warmth and love.
Wordsworth might have pointed to what gain his poetry had
from such experience. Ciardi, perhaps with typically modern
ellipsis, does not make such points in this or the other poems in
Lives of X, but his entire work is there as testimony to what he
had to have gained. Every time he touches the magic Italian subject, his work never fails to come to vivid life.

The conflict with the church is a recurrent motif in the book. It was aggravated by rather stupid-sounding Irish priests in "Two Saints." The nominal difficulty was the death of a childhood friend, Willie Crosby, who appears several times in earlier poems. Willie drowned (in other poems, he caught a fever and died) and because he was not a Catholic presumably went to Hell. Grieving young Ciardi could not attend the funeral because it was in an alien church. When a priest offered the bereaved boy the consolation of "God wanted Willie," his mental response was "And chose *that* way to call him? / Knowing he wasn't even a Catholic? / A boy to murder and then send to Hell?" Through his own experience the boy was up against subtler theological tangles than the priest could or would handle. He was reprimanded in the confessional for his doubts about God's providence; and like a young Huck Finn, he accepted his half-damnation out of a need to assert the deep and sincere individuality. This was his "first heresy." Willie is one of the two saints of the title "because his dying changed my first of reasons."

The other saint is Kiro (Kiroiates), brilliant drinking companion later to be killed on Okinawa, whose possibly sophistical analysis so twisted young Ciardi's guilty obsessions that they became more like benedictions. Kiro even saw the potentialities of a priest in him if circumstances had been different. He wrings from the poet a confession:

> "I wanted to be sane. Saner at least
> than what I'd come from. And I wanted to love.
> Want to. And can. And do. You, among others." (106)

Like Willie he is only "something like a saint," his consequence being "to change me to a good I had once prayed for / and never reached but by the revelation / a man is in the dauntlessness of style."

"The Graph" is a mature reflection on the youthful bravado of the World War II days. He remembers again friends who died and the particular human ironies in their ways of dying, played off against the impersonal background of statistics of several kinds. Various visual effects of bombing and machine-gunning are imaged as points on gigantic graphs. The heart of the poem is an experience close to a visitation to a secular hell. Well into a bottle of whiskey on Okinawa, Ciardi sought shelter from an air raid. It turned out to be a cave or bunker filled with dead men

> . . . where the flamethrowers had left them
> blown back to the inner wall and toppled over
> on one another, sizzled to dry to rot,
> or so I guessed (and maybe sea-air salted). (98)

The drunkenness was perhaps the fittest state in which to receive
this revelation of the human. All of the dead looked alike, with
broken necks and gaping mouths. Recalling it now, the poet puts
it in terms from Dante and Hieronymous Bosch. A rat literally
crawled out of the gaping mouth of one of the mummies. The
sobered soldier left the grisly shelter with a new vision of the
equality of all of the living over the common denominator of
death. He survived the war to complete the dots on the graph of
his own living, but never forgot those dead, "our duplicates and
their own in the globing moon." This would seem to be Ciardi's
version, here in a hideous setting, that any man is fundamentally
everyman. The context is different, but the meaning is close to
Baudelaire's "lecteur, hypocrite, mon semblable, mon frere."

"Epilogue: The Burial of the Last Elder" is an occasion for
Ciardi to appraise once more in a lifetime of it his relation to his
personal heritage which, with the passing of the old relative,
leaves behind it no tangible signs of its existence. It is now all in
the mind and heart of the survivors: "I have nowhere to come
from or return to, / or when I do go back, it isn't there. / The
house is paid for and that's home enough." The ambient political
near-hysteria for the Cause of the moment leads the poet to a
recall of his 1948 campaigning days for Henry Wallace, only to
realize with sixty days to go that "the man was wrong, the Cause
sold"; the result here was an access of understanding that there is
only "the imperfect art of being men." The poem ends with a
kind of benediction in which he wishes for himself "a mercy
beyond recruitment," and for lost everyman who has found no
true home in his life, blessings on his enterprises and the wish that
he seek a meaningful heaven. The last words, suggest a man
alone, accepting his lot in life as value enough: "I have no worlds
to change and none to keep." The American and the existential
worlds become one and the same in this courageous statement.

II   *A Man Grows Older*—The Little That Is All *(1974)*

This volume is mellow, vintage Ciardi, a book steeped in his
own difficult wisdom. Its forty-five poems are grouped in two

sections, thirty-six in "What World It Is" and nine in "Generation
Gap," each section with an epigraph. Nearly every manner and
theme are here, with the possible exception of the vehemence of
some earlier poems, which had returned intermittently in *Lives of
X*. It is typical of a Ciardi collection that his nominal subjects
seem random. There are artist poems ("A Conversation with
Leonardo," "An Apology for Not Invoking the Muse"), family
poems ("Ugliness," "A Poem for Benn's Graduation from High
School"), an ironical love poem ("To a Lovely Lady Gone to
Theory"), urban observations and signs of the times ("On the Or-
thodoxy and Creed of My Power Mower," "Blue Movie," "Generation Gap," "Encounter"), characters ("Kranzfeldt," "Citation
on Retirement"), elegy, satire, fantasy, analogue, intellectual
puzzle and conundrum, and more. In any poem on any subject is
liable to appear a flash of self-awareness seen in perspectives of
time and other modes of being, as in the line, "I wish I could
paint like Degas or believe like Mary." Best of all may be the
redeeming prayer of thankfulness for his not entirely easy lot
("Memo: Preliminary Draft of a Prayer to God the Father"). And
while it is not an entirely new subject, there is a new poignance
over growing older ("Washing Your Feet").

Like Wordsworth, Ciardi can take a subject from everyday life
and present it in such a way as to show its essential strangeness.
Like Hardy and Frost, he can look at something as ordinary as the
death of a bird and reach all the way to philosophical meditations
without being sentimental or ridiculous, for example in "Minus
One": "Whatever remembers us, finally, is enough. / If anything
remembers, something is love." One has a choice of poems no one
but Ciardi could have written in quite this way, the fruits of an
individual sensibility, the plunging emotional nature that has
been long subjected to the analysis of a keen mind and the
discipline of poetic form that is firm without being restrictive,
loose without being slack. A reader could do worse than have his
introduction to Ciardi's work in *The Little That Is All*. Of a
number of poems as provocative as anything he has written, I
choose three for brief attention. They are "An Apology for Not Invoking the Muse," "Letter from a Pander," and "A Poem for
Benn's Graduation from High School."

The first is a serious poem on a serious subject but put in a style
of masculine banter that might be more appropriate for a casual
chippie at a cheap bar than for Erato, muse of lyric and amorous
poetry, who just "popped in." Part of the tension of the poem is

between this language and the meaning of the occasion. Certain
readers might find this vernacular offensive that reeks with one of
the several aspects of Ciardi's "lousy character." Yet to present
the situation in a more conventional manner would be to court
pomposity, a quality this poet is ever the enemy to. The Erato
presented in the poem would prefer it, for she is stuffy. Ciardi has
no less respect for poetry through his playfulness. There is surely a
small irony of self-deprecation (though not much) in his immediate reply to her suspicious query of his activity, "I am
writing an unimportant poem. . . ." On his own he was
scratching "an itch . . . in a minor crease I needn't specify. . . ."
He does not fail to note her beauty in her anger, but pleads his
essential, fallible humanity. He has prayed to be worthy of the
grand ideal she represents and extols, but he cannot transcend his
mutable body and its many contingencies. Important poems are
epics like the *Aeneid* and are properly Calliope's business, he suggests slyly. The poet professes to love the goddess most "for the
sweet small / that trembles to a silence it awakens / and echoes
back a ghost, when you let me say it." When she protests, "You
haven't invoked me in over forty years!" he burns with shame but
offers, "I thought I could say this little on my own, / the way it
happens to us in our smallness." After an imperious glance at his
work of the moment, she departed with harsh words, "See for
yourself what comes of that!" Reading his own work, the poet
despairs:

> How had I dared imagine I might dare
> be only what I am?
>   and yet . . .
>   and yet. . . .[4]

The tension is between the man as he is and the transformation he
undergoes by means of poetry, despite himself. "You tells it to the
music, and the music tells it back to you," Ciardi had borrowed
from the Negro musician twenty years earlier and elaborated it
into a credo of art that revealed a faith in the ability of the right
form to half-create and fully to contain the truth. Ciardi's
haughty Erato might scorn many of the truths thus found, but it
is certain he would not.

"Letter from a Pander" is a meditation on human pretensions
and the proper use of human beings. All things pass, but "no scale

speaks another." "Eternal City," "Immortal Homer," "Countless as stars in the sky," says and sings vainglorious man to a provisional conclusion that seems to be arguing with itself:

> What liars poets are! Toward,
> I suppose, some nerve-truth,
> could they find it to say, as some—
> all the good ones—have. (52)

Being Ciardi, he cannot rest with that but adds "Yet fogged." Both man's mortality and his belief in immortality are endemic to human nature. The poet is not excluding himself from the general condition, for by this point in the poem the pronouns are first-person plural. Could "we endure millennia—will we have learned?" The problem is one of scale, for man rightly considered does have his dimensions of significance. Measured by the right scale, a human greatness "seems possible." Even "love itself may be madness," though by the relativity of scales that could not be true. The poet offers obliquely what truth is possible, "toward neither nonsense / nor always, and on no scale / we are finally sure of. . . ." He speaks as a father to a daughter, out of both relativity and mutability, words "for a boy to say to you / toward his Now and yours / on their own scale." The girl, real or hypothetical, is cautioned to respond gently but subjectively: "Refuse him if he is dull, but not / because he will not love you always. / Nor you, him." The answer she is advised to give to any later interrogations in the name of official values is that "a dead man was your pander, / and loved you as God should." In other words, the subjectivities of the girl and her young man must be measured to their personal scale and not any other. This kind of relativity, far from urging "anything goes," or that all values are equally good and equally bad, insists on the fullest that can be realized, which is always individual and subject to the greatest exercise of choice and responsibility. This is a variation on Ciardi's recurrent position in the midst of the circumambient, unfathomable mystery and the nothingness of life. It seems analogous to the position of the poet who wanted merely to be himself, and yet . . . and yet. . . .

The "Poem for Benn's Graduation from High School" is about the difficulties of a particular parent-child relationship, but partakes of all such. The idiom, though it makes use of the colloquial, is highly individualized. Benn is Ciardi's third child and second son. One suspects from the many essays and poems about him over the years that he is a particular favorite of his father's, who referred to him more than once as the "oaf of my litter." In *Lives of X*, he used the phrase for himself when young. The poem starts with the several-times-repeated situation of an appointment with an assistant principal to see if the school will "keep / him (which no one wants to and sometimes I)," which always comes at "9:00 impossible o'clock A.M." Impossible, that is, for the insomniac and nightworking poet and columnist who has not made it awake to that time in the normal way for over twenty years. (Such habits of work may have seemed as bizarre to the boy as the operatics of an Italian mother had seemed to another boy a generation earlier.) The poet, near to sonambulism, does his fatherly duty and listens to platitudes from the man referred to also as one of the "assistant whomevers," "the assistant whomness," and "this assistant who-bah." The sleep-sodden father gives a glimpse into the fascinating jumble of his free-associating mind. In the official world, the boy, whose difficulties are related to his using marijuana, is "bored incommunicado," while his father is "drafted to boredom and must answer by name, rank, and serial number." Though presented as flat statement of fact, the irony is subtle when the boy, "still sinus-smelling last night's pot, / goes off to his American-Dream-and-After / Seminar." Upon returning home, the father finally dozes off in his chair; when he awakes later, he finds the "difficult" son half asleep in a chair opposite him. To the father's "Well?" comes the reply, "Hello, you old bastard." Like nodding jurors, the father and son have in silence agreed that the petty officials of the world are "guilty of being / exactly themselves." Though nothing else was said,

> There has even been time
> to imagine we have said "Goddamn it, I love you,"
> and to hear ourselves saying it, and to pause
> to be terrified by *that* thought and its possibilities. (83)

Father and son, for all of their different approaches, have been unconsciously agreeing on certain values, the ultimate one of which is surely love. That uttered, pondered, and accepted would be extreme enough in its possibilities to provoke terror, if the concert still held. The assumption in this reading is that the extrapolated love is between the father and son. It might be contended that the terrifying possibilities would result if the pair addressed their love to the assistant officials, but the distance is too great between the values of father and son and those of the others; a tolerance from very nearly another mode of being is all these two can allow the assistants. Curiously, such a reading would make the poem trite, when instead it is a strong poem of family solidity, at least on the part of the father who, obviously much-tried, loves the son as well as the daughter "as God should."

In "Memo: Preliminary Draft of a Prayer to God the Father," the human father moves from one lecture to another, for money, while the members of his family are scattered, the children in different schools, the wife taking care of aged parents. A phone call home relays the news that the younger son "has been busted for pot again. His fourth time." The "reliable fixer" will cost "only another three days on this road." The road, in its extended meaning, "is not what I imagined. It may be better. / Better, certainly, than what I remember from starting." At the end are ironic acceptance and gratitude: "I do not complain: / I describe. I am grateful but imperfect and, therefore, / imperfectly grateful. It is all good enough / / and I thank you, sir." A reader likes the man who wrote these lines, these poems. It is perhaps too much to say Ciardi has never written finer than *The Little That Is All*, but most of his essential qualities are here in probably their most accessible form.

CHAPTER 5

The Translations

DANTE has been one of the abiding interests in Ciardi's life and work. The influence, the inspiration, must be conjectural as to depth and extent, but without a doubt it is real. The fruition is definite, and may be marked by Ciardi's translations of *The Inferno* (1954), *The Purgatorio* (1961), and *The Paradiso* (1970). (The three were published in one volume in 1977 with a new introduction by the translator.) Ciardi's translation of the first five cantos of *The Inferno* appeared in the *University of Kansas City Review* in 1952, but prior to that a portion of Canto V was in *Live Another Day*, and on an adjoining page an original poem called "Letter to Dante." The three books come with a summary of each canto, diagrams, and extensive, if sometimes personal, notes and glosses on the Italian poet, his world, his mind, and the difficulties of making these accessible in the terms of a different time, world, language, and frame of reference. As late as 1972, Ciardi devoted one of his "Manner of Speaking" columns to a problem in Dante,[1] and there had been four earlier ones. All told, the persistence of these efforts represents thirty years of effort in the midst of an extraordinarily busy and productive career. If still conjectural in personal terms, these things speak for the importance of Dante to Ciardi beyond any denial.

Two of the essays in *Dialogue with an Audience*, "How to Read Dante," and "Translation: The Art of Failure," are reprinted in slightly altered form from the *Purgatorio*. In 1955, Ciardi had given a negative review of Dorothy Sayers' *Introductory Papers on Dante* that was at once a well-argued objection to her "missionary impulse" and an implicit justification (when not stronger) of his own approach as translator and as poet himself. For example, "A good poet is not measured by the way he follows doctrine but by the way he survives it into the capture of perceptions that are human rather than doctrinaire."[2] Other Ciardi essays that bear on these themes are the two parts of a long piece, called "The Relevance of Dante," read at the Library of Congress symposium on Dante, May 1, 1965, and reaching a wider audience by appearing in the *Saturday Review*.[3] Not inconceivably they achieve something of what Anthony L. Pelligrini says in a review of Ciardi's *Inferno*: ". . .although it may be read with some profit by the scholar, [it] is not manifestly a scholar's translation. It is aimed, rather, at the general, particularly the American, reader. Its merit, therefore, rests primarily on that basis."[4] The author modestly qualified his essays and translations alike: "That work has not been a scholar's but a poet's work. I am not a Dantean scholar and I must not let myself be betrayed into speaking as one. I am a thief of other men's scholarship, gratefully stealing whatever I can use to make my English version understanding and understandable. Let me believe that scholarship has no better purpose than to make itself available for useful taking."[5] Whether based on borrowed, stolen, or just used sources, Ciardi's work provoked Archibald T. MacAllister to say: "Despite his modest disclaimers of Dante scholarship, his notes as well as his interpretation testify to a profound understanding of the poem on all its levels."[6] In addition to acknowledging the personal advice from eminent Dante scholars, Ciardi lists his chief sources: "For my interpretation of many difficult passages I have leaned heavily on the Biagi commentaries, and even more heavily on the Vandelli-Scartazzini. A number of these interpretations are at odds with those set forth in some of the more familiar English versions of the *Inferno*, but, subject to my own error, this rendering is consistent at all points with Vandelli's range of arguments."[7] This is not to say that Ciardi does not extend, interpolate, and extrapolate. To do otherwise would be to deny the poet in himself. And in essays and translations alike, Ciardi has, in the words of Bernard F. Dick, "rescued Dante from the Malebolge of philology."[8]

Ciardi's translation of the *Inferno* was widely reviewed and generally received with favor, though each critic had his own points to fault. The other two volumes were not reviewed in major journals. More responded to Ciardi's stated ideas about the decisions he had made for his work than to that work itself. Much of the response to the latter was holistic and impressionistic—far from the worst ways in a long poem. A few of the critics went into detail. In general, one suspects that those who respond positively to Ciardi's own poems do the same with his translations, and the same thing is true for the negative.

The major reviewers of Ciardi's *Inferno* were qualified nominally by their knowledge of the Italian original. Most had intelligent objections and preferences on this or that detail or some other interpretation. Most referred to other English translations as a way to make their points for American readers. Despite criticism sometimes carping, but often with points well taken, none (except Hugh Kenner, who preferred the Lawrence Binyon version) failed to see virtues in Ciardi's overall solutions to the project he had embarked upon. Richmond Lattimore commended it as "a real translation, not a free version." Ciardi has given us "Dante translated with reasonable fidelity into an English poem which swings along at a good pace, which is plainer than most English versions and easier to understand. The rhyme is unobtrusive but it is there, and helps." Further, ". . . the whole poem-in-translation is better than its details."[9] MacAllister who at first did not like Ciardi's approximate rhymes soon "realized that these tercets, with first and third lines rhyming, often imperfectly, were carrying the narrative along in much the manner of *terza rima* and with the same relative unobtrusiveness of rhyme as in the Italian. The style, moreover, was plain as much of the 'Inferno' is plain, dramatic where Dante is dramatic, with touches of vulgarity and grim humor to match those of the original which are normally glossed over or unrecognized."[10] Lawrence Grant White in a balanced review concluded that it was "a conscientious and successful translation" and hoped it would be followed by the other parts of the poem.[11] Harry H. Hilborn concluded that ". . . this effort is about as satisfying as any translation of Dante is ever likely to be," and further, "If you must read him in translation, read this one. . . ."[12] And Anthony L. Pelligrini was able to say that ". . . the truth is that this is remarkably faithful for a verse translation. It can also be said that Ciardi's verse, by its notable freshness and definite carrying power, frequently does succeed in recapturing something of the tone of Dante's poem."[13] Years later, in reviewing Mark Musa's translation of the *Inferno*, Bernard F. Dick found Ciardi a necessary comparison: "Only two translators have recreated Dante's peculiar realism: John Ciardi and Mark Musa." Of the two, "Ciardi is clearly the better poet," with the result that "Musa's is a Dantean translation, while Ciardi's is a Dantean poem."[14] Not even the sum total of the critical cavils of these men can nullify their acknowledgement of Ciardi's accomplishment. Ciardi himself pointed out in 1965 that his *Inferno* had sold nearly a million copies in the paperback edition,[15] indicative of its popular success. Despite the absence of critical reviews and the no doubt considerably fewer sales of the *Purgatorio* and the *Paradiso*, there is no reason to think the translations, notes, and commentaries are in any way inferior to the first ones. Since the other sections are more difficult of intellectual access, Ciardi deserves the more praise for his explanations which, whatever the possible scholarly objections, clear up matters for the general reader. If he has read Ciardi's three volumes, his general culture is considerably enhanced.

It is of course an article of faith that no great literary work can be translated without severe losses and things are inevitably added that are not in the original, if only matters of emphasis, of tone. One thinks of Robert Frost's remark that poetry is what is lost in translation, and Randall Jarrell's remark that his German students could not see that Frost was a poet at all. Such opinions as Aldous Huxley's that Poe's poems are better in Mallarmé's translation than in the original are rare. All the problems of taste that exist in the first place with poetry seem to be aggravated when it comes to translations. The reviews of Ciardi's Dante reveal a kind of geologic fault beneath the surface of the American academic terrain. The opposition between scholars and poets in every review is more than a rhetorical convenience. The scholars (whoever they are) like scholarship better than they like poems. Their terms and values are not those of their subject poets, though not wrong thereby. Knowing the original of a translation, they have faint contempt or sometimes pity for those who do not. Poets just as clearly like poetry better than scholarship, and put up with the latter as a part of the existing intellectual world, using it as they will or can, but they resist, at the peril of their creativity, letting it use them. Scholars are secondary and must build on the responses of others; poets are primary and require the firsthand response as a prerequisite of their office. A poet may in fact not be intellectual at all, but a scholar must be. In regard to Ciardi's work on Dante, it is possible to claim that his scholarship could or ought to have led him to different points and interpretations, especially to one's own favorites; but no one can make the case that his are not intelligent, thorough, and thoughtful.

Cruxes remain in Dante after centuries of research and exegesis, and Ciardi has by no means solved them all. The scholars nevertheless have to argue with him on *their* level of attainment, whether or not they have reached his as poet. Interestingly, the most telling objections to his practice come not as a result of his scholarship but of his poetic practice, and not from a scholar but a fellow poet, namely Howard Nemerov.

In the revised edition of *How Does a Poem Mean?* is an appendix containing a section called "Translation as Laboratory." In it is given a simplified version of Ciardi's ideal for a translator's work: "the poem must first of all be a good poem in his own tongue, as if it were originally his poem." And, "probably no test shows a writer's skill in his language so clearly as his ability to build a worthy poem under these circumstances [translation]."[16] As a kind of demonstration, Ciardi gives the first twenty-one lines of Canto I of *The Inferno* in Italian, followed by prose versions of the same lines by Allan Gilbert, and by Charles S. Singleton, and three verse translations—his own and Jefferson Butler Fletcher's, using the same verse pattern, and that of Dorothy L. Sayers. The point is a demonstration and exercise so that students can see what sort of choices have been made and simply how good a piece of writing the poem rendered seems to be in English. "Imagine that what you are reading was written in English as an original poem, and see how it fares," Ciardi advises. Ultimately, students may expect to "come out of it with a clearer sense not only of the problems of language and diction and the sometimes inimical demands of form, but of the nature of poetry as an art form."[17] There is no reason to take the exercise at other than face value. Ciardi's version is not the least considerable. Limitations of space preclude giving the complete passages; perhaps the first six lines will indicate the qualities of each. I have added Laurence Binyon's version for additional comparison. Dante's lines are:

> Nel mezzo del cammin di nostra vita
> mi ritrovai per una selva oscura,
> chè la diritta via era smarrita.
> Ahi quanto a dir qual era è cosa dura
> esta selva selvaggia e aspra e forte
> che nel pensier rinnova la paura!

Gilbert's version, indicated as a measure of the literalness of the others, is: "In the midst of my journey through this life of ours, I was in a dark forest, because I had lost the right road. Oh, how hard it is to tell of what sort this forest was—so wild, rugged, and difficult that as I remember it my fear returns!" Singleton has: "Midway in the journey of our life I found myself in a dark wood, for the straight way was lost. Ah, how hard it is to tell what that wood was, wild, rugged, harsh; the very thought of it renews the fear!" Sayers offers:

> Midway this way of life we're bound upon,
>   I woke to find myself in a dark wood,
>   Where the right road was wholly lost and gone.
>
> Ay me! how hard to speak of it—that rude
>   And rough and stubborn forest! the mere breath
>   Of memory stirs the old fear in the blood. . . .

Ciardi:

> Midway in our life's journey, I went astray
>   from the straight road and woke to find myself
>   alone in a dark wood. How shall I say
>
> what wood that was! I never saw so drear,
>   so rank, so arduous a wilderness!
>   Its very memory gives a shape to fear.

And Fletcher:

> Upon the journey of our life midway
>   I came unto myself in a dark wood,
>   For from the straight path I had gone astray.
> Ah, how is hard the telling what a drear
>   And savage and entangled wood it was,
>   That in the very thought renews the fear!

Binyon for the same lines gives:

> Midway the journey of this life I was 'ware
>   That I had strayed into a dark forest,
>   And the right path appeared not anywhere.
> Ah, tongue cannot describe how it oppressed,
>   This wood, so harsh, dismal and wild, that fear
>   At thought of it strikes now into my breast.

Each of the above renditions has its qualities. The same exercise may be tried at any other point in the poem with about the same results. In the absence of absolutes, a reader may simply take his choice.

Ciardi's two short translator's notes, in the *Inferno* and the *Purgatorio*, give his accounts of the problems encountered and the solutions he found. The first "Translator's Note" is what the reviewers responded to; the much fuller second, though it may be only his response to further work with Dante, may also be taken as his answer to the criticisms of the reviewers, whether or not intended by the author for that purpose. What he has learned about language and poems from his own practice as a poet colors the statements about translation. For all of his reverence for Dante and for poetry, Ciardi as translator is still very much himself and his own kind of poet. The first difficulty he points out is that "each language has its own logic"; thus "transposition" rather than "translation" might be a better name for the process of moving a literary work across the boundary of one language into another. The reason is that translation implies a word for word correspondence from one language to another, which conception is "false to the nature of poetry." The reason is that "Poetry is not made of words but of word-complexes, elaborate structures involving, among other things, denotations, connotations, rhythms, puns, juxtapositions, and echoes of the tradition in which the poet is writing." Presumably, many details perish one way or another in moving from one language to another, but "what must be saved . . . is the total feeling of the complex, its *gestalt*." How is a translation to mean? By trying "for a language as close as possible to Dante's, which is in essence a sparse, direct, and idiomatic language, distinguishable from prose only in that it transcends every known notion of prose." Dante's language is not "the language of common speech," but "a much better thing than that: it is what common speech would be if it were made perfect." (Frankly, one would like this put more exactly.) Dante's language is far from simple, but one of its features is the avoidance of "elegance simply for the sake of elegance." That, and, overwhelmingly, "it is a spoken tongue." Ciardi has "labored therefore for something like idiomatic English" in his rendering. Though foregoing the triple rhyme of Dante's *terza rima* (aba bcb cdc, and so on), Ciardi believes that "some rhyme is necessary," and the three line stanzas seem "absolutely indispensable because the fact that Dante's thought tends to conclude at the end of each tercet (granted a very large number of run-on tercets) clearly determines the 'pace' of the writing. . . ." Even the otherwise-disapproving Hugh Kenner approved Ciardi's definition of "pace" as "the rate at which it [the poem] reveals itself to the reader." One additional point only is needed to give the guiding principles of Ciardi's translation. He has "not hesitated to use a deficient rhyme when the choice seemed to lie between forcing an exact rhyme and keeping the language more natural."[18] The last point especially provoked adverse criticism from reviewers, though it is a common feature of poetry in rhyme-deficient English. Further, it is a characteristic feature of twentieth-century American poetry, which is the language of Ciardi's own poems and the idiom into which he sought to transpose the Italian masterpiece.

Several comments by reviewers who were sufficiently expert in Dante have already been given that bear out Ciardi's success with the overall lineaments and pace of Dante transposed into the American idiom. Nearly everyone objected to a detail or two, but Howard Nemerov may be taken to represent them at their best because his points are made in relation to definite ideas about poetry, which he expresses. Despite Ciardi's evident desire to emphasize qualities neglected in other translations, Nemerov points out, "nevertheless his necessities are the eternal ones which all translators must live with as they may, and we find him, like the others, juggling sense, measure, and sound until he can reach some more or less pleasing compromise." Seemingly, he found Ciardi's modest theoretical claims pretentious, for he is at pains to show that one translator's problems are identical with those of any other. His choice of examples is "merda," which Ciardi has translated "in the approved modern manner, sparse, direct, idiomatic," and justified in a footnote; yet later when the word "sterco" appears, "the need of three syllables instead of one causes him to translate as 'excrement' without footnote, just like Longfellow." The point is "merely that theories of translation spare us none of these decisions."[19]

Nemerov's strongest point comes with his discussion of the "idea of the idiomatic," though it is his sensibility which causes him to reject "a squad of my boys," "no foul play," and "front and center" (Canto XXI) on the grounds that "they don't mix very well." He finds the last not wrong for Dante's "tratti avanti," but to him it conjured up ''the sudden apparition of a hotel clerk.'' Since Ciardi's equivalent is clearly out of the military and the user is one of the Demons, or Malabranche, the point is less than well taken. Nemerov, however, is preparing for a stronger case, namely, ''when idiomatic equivalents do not come easily to hand.'' Ciardi, he says, becomes ''awkwardly literal,'' for instance Guido da Montefeltro's words to Boniface, ''lunga promessa con l'attender corto,'' are rendered literally as ''long promise and short observance,'' despite the fact that ''this expression is neither an English idiom nor even—there is a difference—idiomatic English.'' All of this leads to what for Nemerov is a more important conception of the idea of the idiomatic: ''the idea of the idiom, or style, in which a work is written.'' In elaboration, he states that ''this idea deals with the harmoniousness of expression, the rightness of the relations between expressions, in a single passage or a whole work. . . .'' Here is his most damning indictment. In the sense indicated, he questions whether ''we have here a modern idiom at all, or anything more nearly resembling one than what can be made of a few chance phrases here and there which will give for a moment a modern color to a language otherwise commonplace enough, a language which, seeking an 'idiomatic' equivalent for, say, 'quella lettura' (the one that seduced Paolo and Francesca), falls back upon that high old story.' '' Rather than charging failure directly (though that has to be the intention), Nemerov generalizes his charges into a sort of principle: ''The closeness with which the language of poetry refers to the language of common speech must depend upon the qualities of the common speech; if this be characterless, or effective only from time to time and not continuously, the poetry which refers to it is apt to be patchy, uncertain, and short-winded.'' The critic generalizes even further his negative responses to Ciardi's rhymes and meter. Rather than the reluctance Ciardi indicated, Nemerov regards it as ''headlong eagerness which rimes as follows: spirit / summit, author / honor, lamentation / mountain, council / evil, armpits / circlets.'' Just as clearly, he disapproves of ''those people who do not write free verse but a 'loosened' iambic pentameter.''[20] Since rhythm is one of the supremely constructive principles in Ciardi's theory of poetry and, by extension, of translation and one of the cornerstones of his practice as poet, there is little doubt that Nemerov, disliking the one, would dislike the other. It is not clear which came first.

Upon turning to the close of Ulysses's narrative in Canto XXVI, Nemerov demonstrates certain of his objections to Ciardi's version in detail. He (along with other commentators) objects to the translator's "formal decision to end each canto with a couplet," where Dante had a single line, because it becomes "sometimes an embarrassment, an empty formality" which he wants dispensed with when possible.[21] That is, Ciardi has several times to add his own words to keep his formal commitment intact. The objection is valid, if not overwhelming. Nemerov cites the Longfellow translation, which "at this place is perhaps by no means ideal, but compares favorably with Mr. Ciardi's not least in the allegedly modern virtue of accuracy to the letter." The principle presumably demonstrated is that "subordination and fidelity to the text are as much technical as moral decisions, and though it is often said, nowadays, that the poet-translator is by some mysterious means 'faithful to the spirit of the original,' that is something we can judge of only by his treatment of the letter."[22]

One gathers that Nemerov, at least as critic, prefers tighter rather than looser forms and supreme attention to details, with the result that the poem is a built structure. Ciardi, on the other hand, evidently regards the slightly looser rhythms and rhymes as form enough and at the same time as creative in themselves. Further, they fit into the massive structure of the original. His own practice as poet bears this out. We are very close at this point to a rough opposition in modern terms of Classic (Nemerov) and Romantic (Ciardi).

The first of Ciardi's two longer Dante essays that relate to his translations is "How to Read Dante," which bears especially on the pedagogical aspect of his translations when used as textbooks.[23] It is a synthesis of generally known and accepted modern positions, such as the levels of Dante's symbolism. (It appeared the year Ciardi resigned from college teaching.) There are many observations excellent and well put, such as: "It is true that Dante writes in depth. Though his language is normally simple, his thought is normally complex. But if the gold of Dante runs deep, it also runs right up to the surface." Ciardi the secularist and humanist would need his perspective on so religion-filled a work. As might be expected, Art is the answer: "Dante was a parochial man. He was persuaded that the One Truth had been revealed to him, and he was intolerant of all non-Catholic views. . . . But if the man was parochial, the artist was universal as only art can be. *The Divine Comedy* is a triumph of art over creed. And that triumph—to paraphrase terms that Dante himself might have used—arises from the force of the Aesthetic Mysteries, which is to say, the power of form in the interplay of its structures and its levels of meaning."[24] This point elaborated and illustrated in detail is the gist of the 1965 Dante essay.

"Translation: The Art of Failure" appeared first in October 1961. Essentially, it elaborates the points of the "Translator's Note" of 1954. By this time, *How Does a Poem Mean?* had been published, and some of the points from the textbook are worked into the discussion of the translator's difficulties. Ciardi is modest in his claims; what a translator "tries for is no more than the best possible failure." He gives an account of his experience with his work on Dante that probably would not have satisfied the earlier commentators any better but might have caused them to attack him on different grounds. He "began to peck away at Dante because I could find no translation that satisfied my sense of the original." There is at best the most modest pride in what eventually came out of it: "When I read the original with my rendering in mind I have no choice but to feel sad. When I read any other translation with my rendering in mind, I feel relatively happy. No one, of course, should trust my sense of it, but I must. Who else's sense can I trust?" Thus he strikes the typical personal note that is responsible for much of his value as poet and as translator. He tried strict terza rima, blank verse, terza rima with assonantal rhymes, English couplets, and ballad stanzas, before he hit upon what he designates "dummy terza rima," which he used. It kept the three line units but rhymed only the first and third lines. The values, for himself, at least, were that "what came was reasonably English, reasonably poetry, and reasonably faithful to Dante's pace and to his special way of using language." At least, the translator had a "feeling" of rightness; what followed was "trial and error." After giving some of his trials with a sample passage, he details the errors of his final version as neatly as any hostile reviewer. With so good an intellect as Ciardi's one is suspicious that his final justification may be more for the sake of rhetorical effectiveness than for the sake of truth; on the other hand, it is in keeping with his accounts of his own poems and of the creative process in general: "All I can really argue, as lamely as need be, is that within the essential failure, this final version *feels* enough like the original, and *feels* enough like English poetry (or at least verse) to allow me to conclude that I have probably caught it as well as I shall be able to. . . . What has any poet to trust more than the *feel* of the thing?" It might be possible to put the matter more elegantly, but possibly no more accurately: "Theory concerns him [the poet] only until he picks up his pen, and it begins to concern him again as soon as he lays it down. But when the pen is in his hand he has to write by itch and twitch, though certainly his itch and twitch are intimately conditioned by all his past itching and twitching, and by all his past theorizing about them." For good measure, Ciardi suspects that "any translation turns out to be a long series of such individual cases, each met on its own grounds, and that each is finally settled by *feel*."[25] Let him who will or can gainsay the poet.

The introductory notes, essays, and afterwords, which offer Ciardi's general interpretation of Dante, are primarily intended for pedagogic purposes; the interested reader, the student, and the beginner are their intended audience. The material is remarkably successful in aiding, guiding, leading, cajoling, or just pushing and pulling such readers along. Ciardi's profoundest interpretation of Dante, however, appears in "The Relevance of Dante." Though relatively impersonal in manner, this essay, more than his other writings on Dante, captures the spirit of T. S. Eliot's suggestion of 1950: "Perhaps confessions by poets, of what Dante has meant to them, may even contribute something to the appreciation of Dante himself."[26] In "The Relevance of Dante" Ciardi gives his accumulated "aesthetic wisdom" on the subject of poetry, its methods, its achievements, its grand possibilities. This is what he has gained from a lifetime's devotion to his art. Nor can there be any doubt at this point of the major contribution by Dante to that experience of art. The medieval poet is at once the test and the proof of Ciardi's dedication to his own art. He is, in effect, the vindication of a lifetime's work. Though all the explanation is to give, this is the summary meaning of Ciardi's remark, "I do not read him [Dante] because he is of the fourteenth century but because I am of the twentieth."[27]

Every one of Ciardi's points may be read equally as a statement about his perception of Dante and his own aims in poetry. His first point has to do with Dante's "arduous and ardent vision of Catholicism," which is expressed in "the most monumental metaphoric structure in all European literature." At the same time, a reader need not share the belief in order to appreciate the poem any more than a belief in the gods of Olympus is necessary to read Homer. The reason lies in the nature of metaphor and poetic as opposed to religious communication: "The details are there not as revealed truth but as a guide to truth." Thus, "all men can share with him a view of the nature of man," which is manifested only symbolically in the metaphoric structure of the poem. Because of the "power" of Dante's "personal genius," and "the power of language itself," the poet can "speak in particulars that instantly strike toward universals." The "one enduring reason for reading Dante . . . is for the experience of his vehicle." And Dante achieved "a vehicle of total esthetic possibility." That vehicle includes a "metaphoric structure" which entraps perceptions that could not otherwise have been so much as glimpsed; a "dramatic development" which necessitates "something like a total empathy with every condition of being"; and a "conceptual structure" which interrelates and evaluates the total nature of mankind.[28] In general terms, this is how Dante's poem means.

Whatever the rewards of the conceptual and the dramatic—and Ciardi the critic and translator gives every evidence of understanding them thoroughly—it is Ciardi the poet who says, after explaining the difference between Satan and Medusa, ". . . It is the magnificence of the metaphoric invention that thrills." There is little doubt that "*The Divine Comedy* is the metaphoric, the allegorical, and the musical structure of one man's search not for itemizations from total meaning but for a living esthetic experience of that total." Whether taking God metaphorically or literally, as Dante did, "it is upon God that one's absolute attention must be fixed." For "everything, as Dante labors to make clear, exists in some relationship to God. It follows that one must weigh and value everything in relation to the total." Dante's complex mind and Beatrice's spiritual simplicity are both accorded respect. Whatever Dante turns his mind to allows the reader "to experience mind in the way that is most specific to poetry: in the poet's ability to weigh experience in the balance of art and to assign to each element of the experience, and to its total, exactly the emotional weight we agree should be assigned to it." Both perception and utterance are brought to near-perfection, with the result that a reader's feelings are brought to "precise equivalence." There follows an essentially Ciardian point about Dante and about poetry: "The experience of that equivalence is infallibly an enhancement of our sense of ourselves."[29]

Pleasures in reading Dante include "an enrichment of our sense of language," of course. Even more important is the experience we have of "*mythologized personalities*," which means the various characters, historical or mythical, "reconceived" for the author's own purposes. These personalities when placed carefully by the poet in his "architectonic intricacy" are in "dramatic juxtaposition," the "endless possibilities" of which are "of the essence of mythological power." If our knowledge of mythological Cupid "helps us to dramatize—and thereby to know—our own feelings," how much more a vast "architectural structure of perception" such as Dante's poem![30]

The subtleties of relationship and interrelationship, of parallelism and correspondence in the structure, make the possible revelations in the poem almost endless. Finally, "what this method communicates is a body of knowledge that is both exact and otherwise unknowable. It is that body of knowledge only art can give form to." This knowledge is exact in that the "mythologized personalities" are both "alive in themselves" yet "true to our feelings about ourselves." Also, the great artist "passes value judgments" on the "emotional conditions" he presents. If he is sufficiently great, we concur. Further, "The poet teaches us at an enforcing depth of feeling what we could not otherwise have known about ourselves." Here, Ciardi's interpretation of Virgil becomes especially important: "Virgil is an allegory of the total of knowledge and understanding that a master artist acquires in a lifetime of giving himself to his art." (Or as Sidney Bechet had said, in Ciardi's quotation, long ago, "You tells it to the music and the music tells it back to you.") Human Reason, the usual interpretation of Virgil, is inadequate to convey "multiplicity and simultaneity," though Esthetic Wisdom will suffice.[31]

Following the leads of metaphoric structure, Ciardi offers various incidental insights into the poem. In explaining Virgil's reproof of Dante for his pity in Hell, Ciardi relates our self insights to the poem. Dante "is recognizing a state of being to which he himself might conceivably have fallen." Because God is the "master metaphor of the total Comedy," the souls in Hell are perversions of the human possibilities. Each in fact is "a narrative personality, a theological evaluation, and a metaphor of the possible condition of any man's soul." Dante brings them together in "the theological doctrine of everabounding grace." The souls in Hell, then, have rejected their salvation, have in fact insisted upon Hell "by actively and unswervingly desiring it." Hell,

Ciardi says, "is not *where* the sinners are: it is *what* they are." It is not that they are in Hell, but that "they *are* Hell," which is "a state of being." Ciardi knows the *Inferno* holds fascination for modern man that the other sections do not similarly hold: "Whether or not we know how to say it to ourselves, there is something in the darkness of our age's own mood that responds at great depth to the darkness of Hell." Again, "there can be no question that Hell is our canticle, the idiom of its emotions natively ours."[32] Ciardi wisely does not attempt to explain this situation.

Is it possible that a reasonably good picture of the people who do so respond may be found in the volumes of John Ciardi the poet who reads Dante because he is a twentieth-century man? Without regard for scale, has Ciardi not in his way tried what Dante is the supreme master of? Not only responding to his actual and imaginative life with "a heart of passion beyond most men," but participating in it, he could still see it clearly. What Dante, at least, saw—and what Ciardi surely has tried for—and found a form to contain, is "a total vision of mankind; not a treatise, but an experience of our own identity." All those we meet in Dante "are the populations of our own nervous system." Ciardi obviously values Dante's vision of man's possibilities in relation to his actualities more than he does the specific means by which a person moves from one to the other. Finally, "Dante is relevant because he measures us, and because what we are and value cannot outlive him."[33]

Throughout the study of Ciardi's own poetry, the point must be made over and again that in writing about himself in sufficient depth, perception and form, he attempts to write about men in general. In Dante, he sees how the older poet is writing equally about himself and men in general. The inner is the same as the outer. In Dante's world, the way down is the way up.

Clearly, poets have interests in language and literature that are different from those of scholars. If Ciardi's work with Dante is not enough to make the point, then the essays by Ezra Pound and T. S. Eliot may be adduced to bolster the case. For all their differences, they have many things in common, not least their admiration for the supreme poetic value of Dante, their conviction that he can speak profoundly to twentieth-century man, and the private values he has for each of the three poets.

Eliot makes many points Pound had made earlier, and Ciardi

makes many points both had made. In poetry the three hold many of the same values. All three, in instructing themselves, pass their illumination on to a public, whatever the degree of light vouchsafed. Did Pound influence Eliot? Did both influence Ciardi? Perhaps; even probably. Yet each offers his own insight and emphasis the others lack. It makes just as much sense to say that Eliot builds upon Pound, and Ciardi upon both. That, in fact, is what a tradition is. Be that as it may, Ciardi's essays on Dante can be compared only with those of two of the master poets of our time. In this respect, the company could not be finer.

CHAPTER 6

Overview—Man of Letters in Modern America

WHAT is John Ciardi's place in modern letters? By now in this study, the lines of his accomplishment have been indicated, his best poems named, and cases argued. His thirty-odd books show his attainments as academician, as intellectual journalist, as translator, as writer for children, and of course as poet, the keystone of the arch of his career. His early criticism is enough to show that he could have made an entire career of its practice. It is based upon a thorough knowledge of the history of poetry, qualified by personal tastes, and coupled with the sensitive knowledge of the practice of poetry from the inside. He uses modern methods of analysis, on the whole not original but with new additions of his own and with his own emphases throughout. This strain of his work issues in *Dialogue with an Audience* and the textbook *How Does a Poem Mean?* As translator Ciardi labored for over twenty years to give us three carefully annotated volumes of Dante's *Divine Comedy* translated into a contemporary American form of the language. As reasonable an approximation of the original as any of the others, it seems likely to last as long as this idiom is accepted as a viable language for poetry. As a writer of children's verse, Ciardi is the heir of the great nineteenth-century practitioners Edward Lear and Lewis Carroll; he shares more with Hilaire Belloc than with Walter De la Mare, but little more than bounding rhythms and clever, skillful rhymes with A. A. Milne. To the charge from an affronted sentimentality of violence and cruelty, he gave several answers pointing to the same rationale, one he had tested by the responses of his own three children: "I dislike most of the children's poems I see because they seem written by a sponge dipped in warm milk and sprinkled with sugar. Children as I know them from my own childhood and from my present parenthood, run to violent emotions. One of the best things children's poetry can do is to catch up that violence in the measure and play of rhyme, rhythm, and form—and so make a pleasant, if momentary, assurance of it."[1] The element of social responsibility is typical of him. A reviewer of Ciardi's adult verse pointed to his extreme violence brought under the control of form, and the author acknowledged the truth of both elements. The point here is that the so-called children's verse likely stems from the same creative sources as his other work.

Any of the above would be enough for a separate career, but it is as poet that Ciardi's place must be determined and that he must be vindicated. What, then, is his place? What is the measure? One looks through "standard anthologies," histories of modern American poetry, annual bibliographies, textbooks, and the like, not entirely in vain, for Ciardi is in this one chronologically, that one alphabetically; but he is absent from more than he appears in. If one, two, or even three of the poets of his generation are represented, or just of those included with him in *Mid-Century American Poets* (which he edited), he is not likely to be the choice. Wilbur, Roethke, and Lowell appear in more of the above places than does Ciardi; the same is true of Bishop, Eberhart, Shapiro, Viereck, and Jarrell. The others, Mayo, Scott, Holmes, Schwartz, and Rukeyser, probably less than Ciardi. Further, the reputations of younger poets like James Dickey and James Wright seem to have surpassed Ciardi's. Do these statements indicate, however, anything other than academic accord?

One thing that accidentally or artificially inflates literary reputations is to become the spokesman of popular causes or movements. This happened to some of Ciardi's fellow poets like Shapiro, Viereck, and Lowell, who came into their early maturity with him by mid-century, and a little later to Allen Ginsberg. Not so Ciardi. He has never been the spokesman for anyone except himself, or for any cause but his own. This individuality might make him more nearly the spokesman for Everyman than are the voices of this special interest or that cause. Are any of these reputations, including Ciardi's, in accord with their qualities? Can the enduring ones be predicted, the values that will be late-discovered anticipated? A critic must always be hesitant when it comes to second-guessing the future. Poets, of course, are not in competition, and today's reputation is tomorrow's "post the passing dogs defile" (to adapt Yeats's metaphor).

Ciardi began under the most felicitous of auspices. His first books received praise in prestigious journals from reviewers like Louise Bogan and Louis Untermeyer. Briefly, the poet seemed as bright as any of the new stars in the American poetical firmament, as any of the poets of the mid-century. He had found his most fruitful subjects by the mid-fifties as was shown by *As If*; they were in his Italian background and in the exploration and definition of a modern self, in particular his own. He continued to receive respectful if qualified praise from his fellow poets. Actually, he was appreciated more for his skillful use of poetic techniques than for the solidity of his humanistic position. Watching the antics of the clown, his reviewers failed to see the thoughtful, responsible human being underneath the painted face and baggy pants. His work did not diminish in quality, though he published his best poems side by side with those of lesser quality, like every other poet, and his critical reputation languished. Other than reviews, only three extended essays have been published to this date on Ciardi's work, two of them by the poets Winfield Townley Scott and Miller Williams, who were his personal friends.

Part of the explanation of this decline may be that Ciardi sought and found a sizable middlebrow audience, reaching them in his *Saturday Review* columns and his wide-ranging lecture tours, especially on college campuses. These kept his name before a wide public and no doubt sold his books. He seems to have renounced the highbrow audience and the intellectual critics and joined the many poets who sought to make modern poetry a truly popular and living art. His 1949 essay "To the Reader of (Some) General Culture" had said that such a reader was of more importance to poetry in the long run than Eliot and Pound. Further, he had many sharp things to say in his essays about the failings of higher education (in addition to the witty things he said in his poems), which he left formally in 1961. All of these can smack of the popularizer, the hack, the intellectual prostitute, the man who sold out for money; but there is simply no sign in Ciardi's poetry that he made any special concession or appeal to any audience. There is every appearance that what he wrote was something he would have written because of the poet he was rather than because of the audiences he had. In 1964, he states this position explicitly: "I no longer cling to my sentiments for that reader in quite the same way, though I am sometimes labeled that reader's defender. I don't hate that reader, by any means. But I have to believe the poet owes him nothing. The one thing the poet must observe is his own sense of poetry. He may be right or wrong, but he cannot be right except in his selfish concern for his own sense of the form."[2]

In criticism, the *Unicorn* controversy of 1957 brought together Ciardi's passionate devotion to the art of poetry and his sense of public responsibility, even though it flew deliberately in the face of a predictable, popular opinion—in fact, in the face of many *Saturday Review* readers. Whatever his distance from this audience, and whatever the causes, he has had notable success in reaching it. So Kenneth Rexroth indicated: ". . . John Ciardi is singularly independent, not just of the Establishment, but of literary movements and groups and tendencies. This gives his poetry a human, unliterary quality all too rare in his generation. I once said he looked more like a pilot for Alitalia than a poet, and that is what his poetry is like, the expression of the life and values or a well-educated, widely traveled, man of the world and as such has a far wider appeal than the work of overspecialized sensibilities. A popular lecturer, he has done much to educate the general public in the appreciation of poetry."[3]

If the Romantic values of the new and the original determine the values of art, then Ciardi offers little more than his strongly individual sensibility, for he has created no new ideas or modes or techniques, as did the Imagists, Eliot, or Pound, for example. Rather, he has been comfortable enough in working within the Modernist forms created by others, as were also most of the poets of his generation. He found the inherited forms adequate to contain his creations, despite bulges in every direction. Many individual influences have registered briefly and obviously in his poems and then disappeared, as though the author were testing his own poetic identity by donning others, none of which fitted. Significantly, Ciardi has found the technical means to express his personal vision and to give it wider significance. This has been his lifelong problem as poet, held concomitantly with the faith that it could be solved. He has been more personal in the sense of writing about himself and the things close to his immediate experience than any of his generation. Lowell and Roethke may run him a close second. All such poets have the problem of making themselves count for Everyman, who wants poetry about himself, or that explains himself to himself. On this score, Ciardi has been more successful than have the others. Lowell was aided by his religion, which many share or think they do, and his devotion to causes that touch a segment of popular conscience. Roethke was an intriguing figure because of his bouts with mental illness. The modern reader is acutely aware of problems and aspects of this malady, for it is as well publicized as any commercial product. Did this work offer insight into typically modern dilemmas, if in more acute form? Many read to see. By contrast, Ciardi has not given us the process of personal psychological delving, but rather the results of it, in the sense of the significance to the rational mind. To judge from his poems, Ciardi felt close enough to the pale of sanity in his immediate family circumstances that he struggled for sanity, clarity, full competence. This means, finally, responsibility; supremely so. Frankly, it does not seem that Ciardi's poems have been so valued. Even when he transcended the personal for all to see who would, many saw only the personal.

Early, Ciardi hit on his basic disposition, his role, his angle of vision, and took up his position in the world but not entirely one with it. Though he has clarified, refined, and improved his ability to present his basic themes, there has been no major development in his work, as Eliot moved from doubt to faith and Pound from aestheticism and history to society and economics. Perhaps Ciardi's path is from an implied position to a definitely stated and even reiterated one. In manner his expression, first to last, is in colloquial idiom and rhythms (both too loose for the taste of many critics), with references and metaphors equally out of common life and the world of learning. He has stressed the preeminence of technical accomplishment for poets; but a reader may object that if it is not put to the service of humanly important subject matter, the skills will miss the reader, who wants to take them for granted anyway. Ciardi's skills and means open up an entirely modern subject matter that includes himself yet is bigger than himself. It is that substance that has been insufficiently appreciated and, if poetry is valued, may increasingly be the basis for the enhancement of his reputation—again taking his means, which are at the least adequate, for granted. Briefly, he is a spokesman of the modern doubt, yet he offers an affirmative answer along humanistic lines.

In exploring his developing self (as well as the various provisional selves along the way) and seeking to make it count for others, Ciardi came to the idea that to express the depths of any self profoundly is to express the depths of every self. In brief, this is his faith, and at his best he has nearly achieved his ideal. If he has succeeded, he has reconciled the individual poet with the typical self of the twentieth-century man, whose dilemmas belong to all of us. The solutions for the poet are true or possibly true for us as well. Though posed in a great variety of ways, seen from various angles, given various emphases and modulations, Ciardi's great subject matter grows from his efforts to find a meaning in life. At the most personal level, the writing of poems about the quest may be enough of an answer; but to a reader, the quest and its answer must take other forms. If, on the one hand, Ciardi is the spokesman of the modern uncertainty, if he can find no intellectual justification for life or basis for faith, nevertheless he finds in the experience of life a sufficient underpinning for both acceptance and affirmation. He is willing to take man as he is, life as he has experienced it, and to affirm both strongly. If the presence or absence of God is a mystery too deep for a poet to solve, the mystery of man is sufficient for the poet to probe. His life's work has been to find the forms and the style to contain and express his successive visions of life on these terms. This is the creative center of his poems.

Thus, to a remarkable extent, Ciardi has breached the split at the heart of the modern consciousness. In a world devoid of external certainty, difficult for inner faith, he had made his subjective experience count in the objective world of poetry, where it counts for others as well. If Eliot needed the Church for his solution and Pound needed history and economics, Ciardi tried with his humanity alone, "the sense of what men have in common," as Miller Williams put it. Irony and paradox inevitably prevail in the tenuous bridge Ciardi has built from inside himself to the external world. Perhaps for himself, he has succeeded more than the giants of his parents' generation. He is a remote descendant of Descartes in accepting the experience of the self as his starting point; closer to us, he is a distant cousin of Hemingway in turning the certain defeat of faithless modern existence into a victory for the greater glory of man. He is the pessimist as happy man, the rationalist neither impervious to feeling nor undone by excesses of it. He believes in reason, would like to believe in goodness, looks about him and sees it rarely, then looks within and is still not reassured. Whatever extreme ironies play about his work, they never become cynicism, for here is a man of not-quite faith yet of reconciliation, of acceptance, of affirmation. In him and his work, though mind may dominate here, feeling there, they are on the whole held in a fine and workable balance.

Finally, this affirmation of life, made in uncertainty but not despair, offers a reassuring voice that bears a message less of hope than of something better, namely joy. If the poetry is sometimes didactic, what else could it be with such a "message"? The high aesthetic mode of symbolist poetry has a briefer human history than that immemorial one that seems to instruct while giving pleasure. But Ciardi is also something of an aesthete in values, for he sees the best of a civilization to be in the restraints of, the balance of, disparates, as in art. That is a long way from art for art's sake. Art may come from civilization, but civilization may also come from art—"You tells it to the music and the music tells it back to you." In the correspondences and analogies, how much different is this from the old mystical doctrine that the way down is the way up? In the past, Dante is the supreme artist of these ideas, as Yeats and Eliot are in our time. No doubt there are differences of scope and scale, but Ciardi is of the company.

Of course, these things can be put in a negative way, too. Is Ciardi a major writer, even in the context of those who emerged from the 1940s on? His latest book is equal to his earlier best, but he writes in the minor mode of the short lyric. In contrast to Yeats, who proved what could be done in the form, Ciardi has no major poems, though he has a number of good and valuable ones. He follows the fashion perhaps set by Auden of cultivating the minor because it *is* minor.[4] Despite his claim that to be personal, if one would but go deep enough into the self, is to speak for all of us as well, Ciardi seems often to speak chiefly for himself. Does he not acknowledge it in *The Little That Is All*, and accept it? So, if not about us, then for us? At least we recognize and sympathize with someone we find interesting and if not trust totally still want to know his response. We share it with him. And whether or not it violates an aesthetic principle, we are helped by it. If Ciardi is not original in the sense of creating new forms and modes, he has nevertheless shaped them to fit his own sensibility, which is vigorous and individual. With so dynamic a personality as that in Ciardi's poetry, there is no resting. As he was quoted in *Who's Who in America:* "There is no success. There is only engagement.

Any man who believes he has succeeded has settled for a limited engagement. At any time in one's life there is only the process of engaging more fully. If there is achievement, it is to put by. Achievement is only what brings into view the next thing to be engaged. Stop that process of engagement and the man is stopped dead. Let him go on breathing: he is dead."[5] This remark, in its acceptance of change, its pessimism that nevertheless admits no defeat, its courage, its grim hopefulness, may be taken to stand for the spirit of the best of Ciardi's work. His value lies in the way his work performs just such values.

Notes and References

Preface

1. *Manner of Speaking* (New Brunswick, N.J., 1972), p. 3.
2. "John Ciardi—'Nothing Is Really Hard but to Be Real—,' " *The Achievement of John Ciardi* (Glenview, Ill., 1969), p. 1.
3. "Three Books by John Ciardi," *University of Kansas City Review*, 16 (1949), 119.
4. *Achievement*, p. 1.

Chapter One

1. Olga Peragallo, *Italian-American Authors and Their Contribution to American Literature*, ed. Anita Peragallo (New York, 1949), p. 45.
2. *Manner of Speaking*, p. 10.
3. Peragallo, p. 45.
4. *Twentieth Century Authors: First Supplement*, ed. Stanley J. Kunitz (New York, 1955), p. 200.
5. "John Ciardi: Tufts Poet," *Tuftonian*, 12 (1955), 21.
6. "On Writers and Writing," *Forum*, 3 (1962), 3.
7. *Manner of Speaking*, p. 63.
8. "John Ciardi: Tufts Poet," p. 21.
9. *Manner of Speaking*, p. 63.
10. John Holmes, "A Note on John Ciardi at Tufts," *Tuftonian*, 4 (1944), 122.
11. Ibid.
12. "John Ciardi: Tufts Poet," p. 21.
13. "A Note on John Ciardi at Michigan," *Tuftonian*, 4 (1944), 119.
14. Ibid.
15. "John Ciardi: Tufts Poet," p. 22.
16. Cowden, p. 119.
17. *Manner of Speaking*, pp. 63–64.
18. "A Note on John Ciardi at Tufts," p. 122.
19. *Manner of Speaking*, p. 51.
20. "A Note on John Ciardi at Tufts," p. 122.
21. *Manner of Speaking*, pp. 68–69.
22. *Twentieth Century Authors*, p. 200.
23. "John Ciardi: Tufts Poet," p. 22.

24. *Manner of Speaking*, p. 51.

25. "John Ciardi: Tufts Poet," p. 22.

26. *Twentieth Century Authors*, p. 200.

27. "John Ciardi: Tufts Poet," p. 211.

28. Cowden, p. 119.

29. "John Ciardi: Tufts Poet," p. 22.

30. John Ciardi, "Foreword," *Mid-Century American Poets* (New York, 1950), p. xxv.

31. John Ciardi, *Dialogue with an Audience* (Philadelphia, 1963), p. 13.

32. Ibid., p. 199.

33. Ibid., pp. 16–17.

34. Ibid., p. 117.

35. Norman Cousins, *Present Tense: An American Editor's Odyssey* (New York, 1967), p. 52. In *Dialogue* Ciardi says he "came to SR in January, of 1956" (p.20).

36. *Dialogue*, pp. 21–22.

37. Ibid., p. 18.

38. *Present Tense*, p. 53.

39. "Revamping the *Review*," *Time*, November 22, 1971, p. 62.

40. *Present Tense*, p. 55.

41. Cousins's editorial appeared in the *Saturday Review*, February 16, 1957. It was reprinted in Ciardi's *Dialogue*, pp. 84–87.

42. *Dialogue*, pp. 124–25.

43. Ibid., p. 124.

44. Ibid., p. 139.

45. Reprinted in *Dialogue*, p. 140.

46. *Dialogue*, p. 19.

47. Ibid., p. 157.

48. *Present Tense*, p. 55.

49. *Saturday Review*, November 7, 1970, p. 12.

50. *Saturday Review*, December 12, 1970, p. 24.

Chapter Two

1. "Three Books by John Ciardi," p. 119.

2. John Ciardi, *Homeward to America* (New York, 1940), p. 5.

3. "Introduction: A Man's Voice," *The Selected Poems of John Holmes* (Boston, 1965), p. vii.

4. *Other Skies* (Boston, 1947), p. 10.

5. *Selected Essays of T. S. Eliot* (New York, 1959), p. 243.

6. Ibid., p. 247.

7. Untitled interview with Ciardi in *Counterpoint*, ed. Roy Newquist (New York, 1964), p. 124.

8. "On Writers and Writing," p. 8.

9. *Live Another Day* (New York, 1949), pp. i–ii.

10. *The Inferno* (New Brunswick, N. J., 1954), p. 70.

11. *From Time to Time* (New York, 1951), p. 13.

12. Kenneth B. Sawyer, Jr., "Praises and Crutches," *Hopkins Review*, 5 (1952), 128.

13. Ibid., pp. 128–29.

14. Willard Marsh, "Little Boy Blue and the Beautiful Rose," *Antioch Review*, 12 (1952), 490.

15. *As If: Poems New and Selected* (New Brunswick, N. J., 1955), p. 61.

16. "Graves and the White Goddess—Part II," *Yale Review*, n.s. 45 (1956), 89.

17. "Among the Nightingales," *Antioch Review*, 16 (1956), 116–17.

18. Bernard Brodsky, "Definition of a Wit," *Chicago Review*, 10 (1956), 89.

19. "Among the Nightingales," p. 116.

20. "Poetry," *Saturday Review*, June 21, 1958, p. 43.

21. Ibid., p. 44.

22. John Ciardi, *I Marry You: A Sheaf of Love Poems* (New Brunswick, N. J., 1958), p. v.

23. "Four New Volumes," *Poetry*, 93 (1958), 47.

24. "The Poetry of John Ciardi," *English Journal*, 50 (1961), 587, 589.

25. "Just a Bit of This and That," *Hudson Review*, 11 (1958), 445–46.

Chapter Three

1. Southworth, p. 589.

2. *Counterpoint*, p. 116.

3. "Poetic Violence in Three Parts," *Saturday Review*, April 2, 1960, p. 34.

4. *39 Poems* (New Brunswick, N. J., 1959), pp. 26–27.

5. "Inside a Poem with the Poet," *Think*, September 1958, pp. 20–21.

6. *In the Stoneworks* (New Brunswick, N. J., 1961), p. 36.

7. *Poet's Choice* (New York, 1962), pp. 152–53.

8. "Of Ego," *Saturday Review*, January 22, 1972, p. 25.

9. Burton A. Robie, *Library Journal*, 87 (1962), 4550.

10. "The Wedding of Mercy and Self," *Saturday Review*, March 23, 1963, pp. 78–79.

11. *In Fact* (New Brunswick, N. J., 1962), p. 37.

12. *Person to Person* (New Brunswick, N. J., 1964), pp. 3, 13.

13. Ed. Alex Preminger (Princeton, 1965), p. 847.

14. *Explicator*, 26 (1968), item 28.

15. "A More Comic Spirit," *Poetry*, 106 (1965), 233.

16. "A Five-Book Shelf," *Poetry*, 111 (1967), 187.

17. "Poetic Language," *Hudson Review*, 17 (1964–65), 591.

18. "Poetry and Personal Definition," *Saturday Review*, October 9, 1965, p. 41.

19. *This Strangest Everything* (New Brunswick, N. J., 1966), p. 6.

20. Robert L. Stilwell, *Books Abroad*, 41 (1967), 469.

21. *Choice*, 4 (1967), 820.

22. Stafford, p. 188.

Chapter Four

1. Harry J. Cargas, "Poetry and the Poet: An Interview with John Ciardi," *America*, January 13, 1973, p. 20.

2. Book-of-the-Month Club *News*, June 1971, p. 8.

3. *Lives of X* (New Brunswick, N. J., 1971), p. vi.

4. *The Little That Is All* (New Brunswick, N. J., 1974), p. 27.

Chapter Five

1. "Esthetic Wisdom," *Saturday Review*, April 8, 1972, p. 22.

2. "Dante for the Missionaries," *New Republic*, August 22, 1955, p. 18.

3. "The Relevance of Dante," *Saturday Review*, May 15, 1965, pp. 16–18, 64; May 22, 1965, pp. 51–53.

4. *Modern Language Quarterly*, 17 (1956), 183.

5. "The Relevance of Dante," p. 16.

6. "The Literature of Italy," *Yale Review*, n.s. 44 (1954), 159.

7. "Translator's Note," *The Inferno* (New Brunswick, N. J., 1954), p. x.

8. Review of Dante's *Inferno*, *Saturday Review*, May 22, 1971, p. 38. This review was nominally of Mark Musa's translation, but both Musa and Ciardi received credit for the quoted feat, each in his own way.

9. "The 'Inferno' as an English Poem," *Nation*, August 28, 1954, p. 175.

10. MacAllister, p. 158.

11. "Dante for Americans," *Saturday Review*, September 18, 1954, p. 27.

12. "Italian Literature," *Queen's Quarterly*, 42 (1955), 136.

13. Pelligrini, p. 184.

14. Dick, p. 37.

15. "The Relevance of Dante," p. 16.

16. John Ciardi and Miller Williams, *How Does a Poem Mean?* (Boston, 1975), p. 391.

17. Ibid., pp. 395–96.

18. "Translator's Note," *Inferno*, pp. ix–x.

19. Howard Nemerov, "A Few Bricks from Babel," *Poetry and Fic-*

tion: Essays (New Brunswick, N. J., 1963), p. 362. The essay originally appeared in the *Sewanee Review* in 1954.

20. Ibid., pp. 362–63.

21. Ibid., p. 364.

22. Ibid., p. 365.

23. The introductory essay to the one-volume edition, "The Method of *The Divine Comedy,"* is likewise intended for the beginner. The only new thing in it is Ciardi's very great admiration for *The Paradiso;* in particular, he admires "Dante's ability to outsoar all previous dimension of expectation" in the "inexhaustability" of his inventiveness, making *The Paradiso* the "supreme achievement of western literature," in fact, beyond that, "the summit of all European expression." *The Divine Comedy* (New York, 1977), pp. xvi–xvii.

24. "How to Read Dante," *Dialogue with an Audience*, pp. 270, 275–76.

25. *Dialogue*, pp. 281, 284, 288.

26. "What Dante Means to Me," *To Criticize the Critic and Other Writings* (New York, 1965), p. 125.

27. "The Relevance of Dante," p. 17.

28. Ibid., pp. 16–17.

29. Ibid., p. 18.

30. Ibid., p. 64.

31. "The Relevance of Dante," Part II, pp. 51–52.

32. Ibid., pp. 52–53.

33. Ibid., p. 53.

Chapter Six

1. "WLB Autobiography: John Ciardi," *Wilson Library Bulletin*, 38 (1964), 481.

2. Ibid., p. 482.

3. *American Poets in the Twentieth Century* (New York, 1971), p. 124.

4. David Perkins, *A History of Modern Poetry: From the 1890s to the High Modernist Mode* (Cambridge, Mass., 1976), p. 7.

5. *Who's Who in America*, 1976 ed., p. 573.

Selected Bibliography

PRIMARY SOURCES

1. Poems

As If: Poems New and Selected. New Brunswick, N. J.: Rutgers University Press, 1955.
From Time to Time. New York: Twayne, 1951.
Homeward to America. New York: Henry Holt, 1940.
I Marry You: A Sheaf of Love Poems. New Brunswick, N. J.: Rutgers University Press, 1958.
In Fact. New Brunswick, N. J.: Rutgers University Press, 1962.
In the Stoneworks. New Brunswick, N. J.: Rutgers University Press, 1961.
Limericks: Too Gross. With Isaac Asimov. New York: W. W. Norton, 1978.
The Little That Is All. New Brunswick, N. J.: Rutgers University Press, 1975.
Live Another Day. New York: Twayne, 1949.
Lives of X. New Brunswick, N. J.: Rutgers University Press, 1971.
Other Skies. Boston: Little, Brown, 1947.
Person to Person. New Brunswick, N. J.: Rutgers University Press, 1964.
39 Poems. New Brunswick, N. J.: Rutgers University Press, 1959.
This Strangest Everything. New Brunswick, N. J.: Rutgers University Press, 1966.

2. Selection

The Achievement of John Ciardi. Ed. Miller Williams. Glenview, Ill.: Scott, Foresman, 1969. The poems are selected from *Other Skies* through *This Strangest Everything.* Williams's introduction, "John Ciardi—'Nothing Is Really Hard But To Be Real,' " is the best essay on Ciardi to date.

3. Translations

The Divine Comedy. By Dante Alighieri. New York: W. W. Norton, 1977. A one-volume edition with a new introduction by the translator.
The Inferno. By Dante Alighieri. Historical introduction by A. T. MacAllister. New Brunswick, N. J.: Rutgers University Press, 1954. Reprinted in paperpack by the New American Library, 1954.

180

The Paradiso. By Dante Alighieri. Introd. by John Freccero. New York: New American Library, 1970.
The Purgatorio. By Dante Alighieri. Introd. by Archibald T. MacAllister. New York: New American Library, 1961.

4. Juveniles
An Alphabestiary. Philadelphia: J. B. Lippincott, 1967.
Fast and Slow. Boston: Houghton Mifflin, 1975.
I Met a Man. Boston: Houghton Mifflin, 1961. New ed., 1973.
John J. Plenty and Fiddler Dan: A New Fable of the Grasshopper and the Ant. Philadelphia: J. B. Lippincott, 1963.
The King Who Saved Himself from Being Saved. Philadelphia: J. B. Lippincott, 1965.
The Man Who Sang the Sillies: Poems. Philadelphia: J. B. Lippincott, 1961.
The Monster Den. Philadelphia: J. B. Lippincott, 1966.
The Reason for the Pelican. Philadelphia: J. B. Lippincott, 1959.
Scrappy the Pup. Philadelphia: J. B. Lippincott, 1960.
Someone Could Win a Polar Bear. Philadelphia: J. B. Lippincott, 1970.
The Wish Tree. New York: Crowell-Collier, 1962.
You Know Who. Philadelphia: J. B. Lippincott, 1965.
You Read to Me, I'll Read to You. Philadelphia: J. B. Lippincott, 1962.

5. Essays
Dialogue with an Audience. Philadelphia: J. B. Lippincott, 1963.
Manner of Speaking. New Brunswick, N. J.: Rutgers University Press, 1972.

6. Textbooks
How Does a Poem Mean? Boston: Houghton Mifflin, 1959; rev. ed. with Miller Williams, 1975.
Poetry: A Closer Look. With James M. Reid and Laurence Perrine. New York: Harcourt, Brace. 1963.

7. Editions
Mid-Century American Poets. New York: Twayne, 1950.

8. Interviews and Essays on His Own Work
Ciardi has many essays that bear on his work, such as the "Foreword to the Reader of (Some) General Culture" in *Live Another Day* and the "Translator's Note" in the *Inferno* and the *Purgatorio*. The first is reprinted in *Mid-Century American Poets*; the third is in *Dialogue with an Audience*. Remarks on his own work are scattered throughout his essays, a great many of which have not been collected. Listed here are essays and interviews that are important for the study of his work.

Ciardi is particularly good as a commentator on his own work. The essays are also valuable for the ideas on poetry in general.

Counterpoint. Ed. Roy Newquist. New York: Rand McNally, 1964. Interview by the editor in March 1964.

"Inside a Poem with the Poet," *Think*, September 1958, pp. 20–21. On "Bridal Photo, 1906," from *39 Poems*.

"On Writers and Writing," *Forum*, 3 (1962), 3–12. Replies to questions put by graduate students at Ball State Teachers College in June 1961.

"Poetic Violence in Three Parts," *Saturday Review*, April 2, 1960, p. 34. On *39 Poems*.

"Poetry," *Saturday Review*, June 21, 1958, pp. 43–44. On *I Marry You*.

"Poetry and Personal Definition," *Saturday Review*, October 9, 1965, p. 41. A "Manner of Speaking" column prepared at the prompting of William J. Martz and included in his *The Distinctive Voice: Twentieth Century American Poetry*, Glenview, Ill: Scott, Foresman, 1966.

"Poetry and the Poet: An Interview with John Ciardi," by Harry J. Cargas, *America*, January 13, 1973, pp. 18–20. Cargas supplied only the questions.

Poet's Choice. Ed. Paul Engle and Joseph Langland. New York: Dial Press, 1962, pp. 150–53. Analysis of "Song for an Allegorical Play," from *In the Stoneworks*.

"WLB Autobiography: John Ciardi," *Wilson Library Bulletin*, 38 (1964), 480–82. Not primarily on the work but valuable none the less for the poet's views.

9. Recordings

About Eskimos, and Other Poems. Spoken Arts, 1974. SAC 6103.

As If. Folkways Records, 1956. FL 97–80. Recorded at Rutgers University, 1955.

Contemporary American Poets Read Their Work: John Ciardi. Everett / Edwards Cassette 165.

Dante's Inferno. Folkways Records, 1954. FP 97–1. Ciardi reads the first eight cantos of his translation.

I Met a Man. Pathways of Sound, 1962.

Introduction to Poetry. Everett / Edwards Cassette 844.

The King Who Saved Himself from Being Saved. Spoken Arts, 1971. SAC 6053. Contains ten poems besides the title poem.

Recording of Poets Reading Their Own Poems: John Ciardi and W. D. Snodgrass. Library of Congress, Division of Music, 1961. Recorded in New York City, April 20, 1955.

Someone Could Win a Polar Bear, and Other Poems. Spoken Arts, 1972. SA 1102. Spoken Arts, 1974. SAC 6102.

Spoken Arts Treasury of 100 American Poets Reading Their Poems, v. 13. Spoken Arts, 1969. SA 1052.

This Strangest Everything. Spoken Arts, 1967. SA 956–947. Recorded at Rutgers University, 1966.

What Do You Know About Poetry? An Introduction to Poetry for Children. Spoken Arts, 1974. SAC 6101.

What Is a Poem: A Discussion of How Poems Are Made. Spoken Arts, 1974. SA 1115.

Why Noah Praised the Whale, and Other Poems. Spoken Arts, 1974. SAC 6104.

You Know Who. John J. Plenty and Fiddler Dan and Other Poems. Spoken Arts, 1966. SA 914. Spoken Arts, 1969. SAC 6038.

You Read to Me, I'll Read to You. Spoken Arts, 1962. SA 835. Read by the poet and his children.

SECONDARY SOURCES

1. Bibliography

WHITE, WILLIAM. *John Ciardi: a Bibliography.* With a note by John Ciardi. Detroit: Wayne State University Press, 1959. By no means complete, even within its time limits, but still a valuable compilation which suggests the wide range of Ciardi's literary activities. Lists many items not to be found in the periodical guides.

2. Parts of Books and Essays on Ciardi

There is no other book-length study of Ciardi to date. The comprehensive essays, each partial but valuable for the overall study of the poems, are by Scott, Southworth, and Williams in *The Achievement of John Ciardi* (see No. 2 above). The piece by Hughes is nominally a review of *Lives of X* but has much wider implications. Of the many reviews of Ciardi's books, only those are cited which go beyond the nominal subject in significance.

COUSINS, NORMAN. *Present Tense: An American Editor's Odyssey.* New York: McGraw-Hill, 1967.

COWDEN, ROY W. "A Note on John Ciardi at Michigan," *Tuftonian* 4 (1944), 118–19.

DICK, BERNARD F. Rev. of Dante's *Inferno*, trans. by Mark Musa, *Saturday Review*, 54 (May 22, 1971), 37–38. Valuable, if brief, comparison of Musa and Ciardi translations.

GROFF, P. J. "Transformation of a Poet: John Ciardi," *Horn Book*, 40 (April 1964), 1953–54. Negative account of Ciardi's first five children's books.

HALL, DONALD. "The New Poetry: Notes on the Past Fifteen Years in America," *New World Writing: Seventh Mentor Selection.* New York: New American Library, 1955. Calls Ciardi one of the "Wurlitzer Wits" because of the variety of everyday objects and scenes in his work.

HOLMES, JOHN. "A Note on John Ciardi at Tufts," *Tuftonian*, 4 (1944), 122.

———. "John Ciardi: Tufts Poet," *Tuftonian*, 12 (1955), 21–24.

HUGHES, JOHN W. "Humanism and the Orphic Voice," *Saturday Review*, May 22, 1971, pp. 31–33. [See headnote.]

KENNER, HUGH. "Problems in Faithfulness and Fashions," *Poetry*, 85 (1955), 225–31. Compares Binyon and Ciardi translations of the *Inferno*.

LAING, DILYS. "Some Marrying and Some Burning," *Nation* (September 13, 1958, pp. 137–39. A review of *I Marry You* that makes points about Ciardi's practice in general.

LATTIMORE, RICHMOND. "The 'Inferno' as an English Poem," *Nation*, August 28, 1954, p. 175. Good, brief critical appraisal.

MACALLISTER, ARCHIBALD T. "The Literature of Italy," *Yale Review*, n. s. 44 (1954), 155–59.

NEMEROV, HOWARD. *Poetry and Fiction: Essays*. New Brunswick, N. J.: Rutgers University Press, 1963. "A Few Bricks from Babel" includes a review of Ciardi's translation of the *Inferno;* it appeared originally in the *Sewanee Review* in 1954.

PERAGALLO, OLGA. *Italian-American Authors and Their Contribution to American Literature*. Ed. by Anita Peragallo. New York: S. F. Vanni, 1949.

SCOTT, WINFIELD TOWNLEY. "Three Books by John Ciardi," *University of Kansas City Review*, 16 (1949), 119–25. The books are Ciardi's first three volumes.

SOUTHWORTH, JAMES G. "The Poetry of John Ciardi," *English Journal*, 50 (1961), 583–89. Consideration of the volumes through *39 Poems* by an academic who was also a good critic.

SPENDER, STEPHEN. "Poetry vs. Language Engineering," *New Republic*, August 15, 1960, pp. 17–18. Questions much of Ciardi's approach to poetry in *How Does a Poem Mean?*

WHITE, LAWRENCE GRANT. "Dante for Americans," *Saturday Review*, September 18, 1954, pp. 13, 27.

Index

185